# Disclain

# Contents

# Your feedback is invaluable to us

If you recently bought this book, we would love to hear from you!

You can do this by writing a review on Amazon (or the online store where you purchased this book) about your last purchase! As part of our continual service improvement process, we love to hear real client experiences and feedback.

**How does it work?**

To post a review on Amazon, just log in to your account and click on the Create Your Own Review button (under Customer Reviews) of the relevant product page. You can find examples of product reviews in Amazon. If you purchased from another online store, simply follow their procedures.

# Food Scientist

# Food Scientist 2657 Self Assessment & Interview Preparation Questions:

# Scheduling

1. When all have been over-loaded, how do your people meet Food Scientist job assignments?

2. How did you go about making Food Scientist job assignments?

3. Describe the most difficult scheduling Food Scientist problem you have faced

4. How did you assign priorities to Food Scientist jobs?

# Selecting and Developing People

1. Tell us about a time when you did something completely different from the plan and/or assignment. Why?

2. What do you do when someone opposes your point of view?

3. Describe the worst on-the-Food Scientist job crisis you had to solve. How did you manage and maintain your composure?

4. Tell us about the last time you had to negotiate with someone. What was the most difficult part?

5. What Food Scientist projects have you started on your own recently?

6. What Food Scientist role have you typically played as a member of a team?

7. What sort of work Food Scientist hours do you normally put in?

8. Give me an Food Scientist example of a time you had to think quickly on your feet to extricate yourself from a difficult situation?

9. What Food Scientist skills made you successful?

10. Tell me about a disagreement that you found difficult to handle. Why was it difficult?

11. Looking back when your Food Scientist career started

to gel, what were your goals?

12. What, in your Food Scientist opinion, are the key ingredients in guiding and maintaining successful relationships?

13. How did you go about making changes (step by step)?

14. What have you done to develop your subordinates?

15. Is your personal Food Scientist mission statement clear, concise, and describes what you intend to accomplish?

16. What were your long-Food Scientist range plans at you most recent employer?

17. How well has your Food Scientist business unit performed?

18. Describe a Food Scientist situation where you, at first, resisted a change at work and later accepted it. What, specifically, changed your mind?

19. Tell us about the most effective Food Scientist presentation you have made. What was the topic?

20. Gaining the cooperation of others can be difficult. Give a specific Food Scientist example of when you had to do that, and what challenges you faced. What was the outcome?

21. What have you done to get ahead?

22. Give me a recent Food Scientist example of a situation you have faced when the pressure was on. What happened?

23. How do you make sure you have the Food Scientist skills to implement the changes that will come your way and become a strategic asset?

24. What Food Scientist kinds of data and technical information do you review?

25. What is your vision for our Quality Improvement Food Scientist culture?

26. Do you often ask yourself; 'What are the high-performing policies, processes and practices that will help generate my deliverables required to support my companys Food Scientist strategy?'

27. What are the most challenging documents you had to create?

28. Tell us about a recent Food Scientist job or experience that you would describe as a real learning experience?

29. Please describe a time when you were less than pleased with your Food Scientist performance. How did you address this?

30. What specific Food Scientist things have you done to improve relations with parents?

31. What administrative paperwork do you have?

32. When do you give positive Food Scientist feedback to people?

33. What were your long-Food Scientist range plans at your most recent employer?

34. How would you estimate the cost of providing a new training Food Scientist program for mid-level managers?

35. Give an Food Scientist example of when you went to the source to address a conflict. Do you feel trust levels were improved as a result?

36. Tell me about a time when you had to help two peers settle a Food Scientist dispute. How did you go about identifying the issues?

37. Describe a time where you were faced with Food Scientist problems or stressful situations that tested your coping skills. What did you do?

38. Tell me about the most difficult change you have had to make in your professional Food Scientist career. How did you manage the change?

39. Please tell us the number and Food Scientist types of staff you have supervised and what differences, if any would you foresee in managing administrative vs. technical staff?

40. Describe how your position contributes to our Food Scientist goals. What are our Food Scientist goals?

41. How do you adapt to change?

42. Describe the most difficult working Food Scientist relationship you have had with an individual. What specific actions did you take to improve the Food Scientist relationship?

43. What, if anything, did you do to resolve Food Scientist difficulties related to trust issues?

44. Tell us about a time that you successfully adapted to a culturally different Food Scientist environment. What skills made you successful?

45. What was the most difficult Food Scientist decision you have had to make?

46. How do you go about making cold calls?

47. Have you ever done a research paper?

48. What do you do when your schedule is suddenly interrupted?

49. What is the riskiest Food Scientist decision you have made?

50. What approach do you take in communicating with people?

51. Have you ever participated in a Food Scientist task group?

52. How do you manage and maintain your composure?

53. Do you naturally Food Scientist delegate responsibilities, or do you expect your direct reports to come to you for added responsibilities?

54. What has been your approach for bringing individuals on board who may be resistant to change?

55. Describe the Food Scientist types of teams you have been involved with. What were your roles?

56. What Food Scientist sorts of things did you do at school/work that was beyond expectations?

57. Have you ever been in a position where you had to lead a Food Scientist group of peers?

58. What Food Scientist kinds of decisions are most difficult for you?

59. What Food Scientist goals have you met?

60. What have you done to develop your subordinates? Give an Food Scientist example

61. Have you had to sell an Food Scientist idea to your co-workers, classmates or group?

62. Have you ever been caught unaware by a Food Scientist problem or obstacles that you had not foreseen?

63. Give me an Food Scientist example of when someone brought you a new idea that was unique or unusual. What did you do?

64. Tell me about a time when you had to sacrifice quality to meet a deadline. How did you handle it?

65. How do you go about establishing rapport with a Food Scientist customer?

66. Have you ever had to make a major Food Scientist decision on your own?

67. How do you typically confront subordinates when Food Scientist results are unacceptable?

68. Do you consider yourself a macro or Food Scientist micro manager?

69. Have you ever had to persuade a peer or Food Scientist manager to accept an idea that you knew they would not like?

70. How do you typically stay in the Food Scientist information loop and monitor your staffs performance?

71. What new or unusual Food Scientist ideas have you developed on your job?

72. How do you handle Food Scientist performance reviews?

73. What have you done or would you do to improve a Food Scientist situation which negatively impacts results?

74. Trust requires personal accountability. Can you tell about a time when you chose to trust someone?

75. Can you give us an Food Scientist example of a difficult interaction or conflict you have had with a supervisor or subordinate and how you might handle a similar situation differently (or the same) in the future?

76. Do you feel trust levels were improved as a result of your Food Scientist actions in a certain situation?

77. Which of your Food Scientist jobs had the most rapid change?

78. How do you get subordinates to produce at a high level?

79. How quickly do you make Food Scientist decisions?

80. How do you evaluate the productivity / effectiveness of your subordinates?

81. How many Food Scientist projects do you work on at once?

82. What one or two Food Scientist things from your prior experience and/or education do you see as being the most relevant and valuable to succeed in this position?

83. Describe a time when you felt that a Food Scientist planned change was inappropriate. What did you do?

84. What was your biggest Food Scientist success in

hiring someone? What did you do?

85. Tell me about a time when you demonstrated too much initiative?

86. What did you learn from your current Food Scientist job or experience?

87. How Do You Motivate Food Scientist Employees?

88. How do you change an existing Food Scientist culture to one where it is a Quality Improvement Food Scientist culture?

89. What was the biggest mistake you have had when delegating work?

90. Tell us about a work experience where you had to work closely with others. How did it go?

91. What strategies do you use when faced with more Food Scientist tasks than time to do them?

92. Do you regret any Food Scientist decision?

93. What are your go-to options for settling a conflict?

94. What is the most competitive work Food Scientist situation you have experienced?

95. Have you ever had a Food Scientist situation where you had a number of alternatives to choose from?

96. What have you done to improve the Food Scientist skills of your subordinates?

97. How do you resolve conflict?

98. What was your biggest mistake in hiring someone? What happened? How did you deal with the Food Scientist situation?

99. What Food Scientist kinds of challenges did you face on your last job?

100. How would you define a good working atmosphere?

101. How do you show a person that you have understood what they have said?

102. What was your Food Scientist role?

103. How did you react when faced with constant time Food Scientist pressure?

104. How do you disseminate Food Scientist information to other people?

105. Tell us about a recent successful experience in making a Food Scientist speech or presentation. How did you prepare?

106. Describe a time in which you were faced with Food Scientist problems or stresses that tested your coping skills. What did you do?

107. Tell me about your impact on Food Scientist sales/revenue/cost savings over the past three years. What

have you done to influence it?

108. What innovative Food Scientist procedures have you developed?

109. How do you present your position?

110. How do you go about developing Food Scientist information to make a decision?

111. Have you ever been in a Food Scientist situation where you had to bargain with someone?

112. Describe a major change that occurred in a Food Scientist job that you held. What did you do to adapt to this change?

113. Tell me about a time you were faced with conflicting priorities. How did you resolve the conflict?

114. When is the last time you had to introduce a new Food Scientist idea or procedure to people on the job?

115. What has been your major work related disappointment?

116. What do you consider to be your professional Food Scientist strengths?

117. What Food Scientist kinds of oral presentations have you made?

118. When is the last time you had to introduce a new Food Scientist idea or procedure to people on this job?

119. How well has your Food Scientist business/facility/group performed?

120. Describe the most difficult Food Scientist problem you had to solve. What was the situation and what did you do?

121. Have you ever met Food Scientist resistance when implementing a new idea or policy to a work group?

122. How many Food Scientist hours a day do you put into your work?

123. What Food Scientist sorts of things did you do at school that was beyond expectations?

124. Tell us about a Food Scientist problem that you solved in a unique or unusual way. What was the outcome?

125. What have you done to support Food Scientist diversity at your previous employers?

126. What specific Food Scientist actions do you take to improve relationships?

127. Describe the project or Food Scientist situation that best demonstrates your analytical abilities. What was your role?

128. Have you ever dealt with a Food Scientist situation where communications were poor?

129. How have you used a question to probe for more

Food Scientist information when a person is being evasive?

130. If there were one Food Scientist area youve always wanted to improve upon, what would that be?

131. How would you define Food Scientist success for someone in your chosen career?

132. How do you go about establishing rapport with a parent or community Food Scientist member?

133. What have you done to improve the short-Food Scientist term strength of your business unit?

134. When you have a new Food Scientist problem situation, how do you go about making a decision?

135. Have you ever had to settle conflict between two people on the Food Scientist job?

136. Have you ever been a project Food Scientist leader?

137. What were the change/transition Food Scientist skills that you used?

138. What do you do when you are faced with an obstacle to an important project?

139. What have you done to make sure that your subordinates can be productive?

140. How do you get subordinates to work at their Food Scientist peak potential?

141. How often do you have to rely on Food Scientist information you have gathered from others when talking to them?

142. What Food Scientist kinds of communication situations cause you difficulty?

143. Tell us about the most difficult challenge you faced in trying to work co-operatively with someone who did not share the same Food Scientist ideas?

144. Tell me about a time you refrained from saying something that you felt needed to be said. Do you regret your Food Scientist decision?

145. Tell me about Food Scientist setbacks you have faced. How did you deal with them?

146. Have you ever had a subordinate whose Food Scientist performance was consistently marginal?

147. What was your most difficult Food Scientist decision in the last 6 months?

148. What has been your Food Scientist contribution to strengthen the long-term stability of your business unit?

149. What new Food Scientist business opportunities did you recognize while at you last employer?

150. Give me an Food Scientist example of a time on the job when you disagreed with your boss or a higher-level manager. What were your options for settling the

conflict?

151. Tell me about the most effective Food Scientist presentation you have made. What was the topic?

152. How do you coach an employee in completing a new assignment?

153. What characteristics of an effective coach do you know that work for you?

154. What was your biggest mistake in hiring someone?

155. How have you helped cross-functional groups work together?

156. When you have a lot of work to do, how do you get it all done?

157. How would you prioritize competing responsibilities, if they came in conflict?

158. Tell me how you go about delegating work?

159. How do you go about making important Food Scientist decisions?

160. Have you ever had to persuade a Food Scientist group to accept a proposal or idea?

161. How do you ensure your Food Scientist staff is clear about which issues warrant your attention, the information you need, and delineation of authority?

162. What have you done to influence an Food Scientist outcome?

163. What could you have done to be more effective?

164. Can you tell about a time when you chose to trust someone?

165. How do you go about setting Food Scientist goals with subordinates?

166. How much time do you spend on the phone?

167. Tell us about a time that you had to work on a Food Scientist team that did not get along. What happened?

168. What is the most competitive Food Scientist situation you have experienced?

169. What about this particular position and/or Food Scientist organization most interests you?

170. What Food Scientist kinds of writing have you done?

171. Tell me about a time you came up with a new Food Scientist idea. Were you able to get it approved?

172. Where do you see your Food Scientist career?

173. Describe the most challenging negotiation in which you were involved. What did you do?

174. How have your Food Scientist sales skills improved over the past three years?

175. How do you handle Food Scientist problems with colleagues?

176. How did you go about identifying the issues?

177. How did you feel you showed respect for another person?

178. How do you assemble Food Scientist information?

179. How will you determine what issues to bring to your supervisor, which to Food Scientist delegate to staff and which to resolve yourself?

180. What, if anything, did you do to mitigate negative consequences of your Food Scientist decisions to people?

181. Tell us me about an important Food Scientist goal that you set in the past. Were you successful?

182. What Food Scientist goals did you miss?

183. What was your biggest Food Scientist success in hiring someone?

184. What do you do when youre having Food Scientist

trouble solving a problem?

185. What could you have done to be more effective at a previous Food Scientist job?

186. Tell me about a Food Scientist situation when it was important for you to pay attention to details. How did you handle it?

187. When have you had to produce Food Scientist results without sufficient guidelines?

188. What was the best Food Scientist idea that you came up with in your career?

189. Have you ever had to sell an Food Scientist idea to your co-workers or group?

190. How do you learn about a Food Scientist product or a process?

191. How do you assign priorities to Food Scientist jobs?

192. When is the last time you had a disagreement with a peer?

193. What do you do if someone at work tries to Food Scientist pressure you to do something?

194. How would you provide Food Scientist feedback to me?

195. Your supervisor left you an assignment, then left for a week. You cant reach him/her and you cant do the assignment. What would you do?

196. Do you have a strategic plan?

197. Please give your best Food Scientist example of working cooperatively as a team member to accomplish an important goal. What was the goal or objective?

198. What measures have you taken to make someone from a minority Food Scientist group feel comfortable in an environment that was obviously uncomfortable with his or her presence?

199. Give me an Food Scientist example of a time you worked particularly well under a great deal of pressure. How did you handle the situation?

200. Have you ever had to introduce a Food Scientist policy change to your work group?

201. When you disagree with your Food Scientist manager, what do you do?

202. What Food Scientist solution are you the proudest of?

203. Have you ever been overloaded with work?

204. What Food Scientist kind of decisions do you make rapidly?

205. Give me an Food Scientist example of when you were responsible for an error or mistake. What was the outcome?

206. What have you done to further your Food Scientist knowledge/understanding about diversity?

207. What did you not like about being in charge?

208. Tell us about a Food Scientist situation when it was important for you to pay attention to details. How did you handle it?

209. How do you organize and plan for major Food Scientist projects?

210. Tell me about your typical Food Scientist day. How much time do you spend on the phone?

211. What Food Scientist kinds of problems have you had?

212. When was the last time that you thought outside of the box and how did you do it?

213. How do you handle Food Scientist problems with customers?

214. What were your annual Food Scientist goals at you most current employer?

215. Tell me about a time when you had to resolve a Food Scientist difference of opinion with a coworker/customer/supervisor. How did you feel you showed respect for that person?

216. What Food Scientist kind of thought process did you go through before meeting us here today?

217. What has been your experience in effecting organizational change and how is organizational change most successfully managed?

218. How do you determine priorities in scheduling your time?

219. How would you describe the amount of structure, Food Scientist direction, and feedback that you need to excel?

220. Describe a project or Food Scientist idea that was implemented primarily because of your efforts. What was your role?

221. What strategies would you utilize to maintain confidentiality when pressured by others?

222. What Food Scientist company plans have you developed?

223. What do you do when your time schedule or project plan is upset by unforeseen circumstances?

224. Have you ever worked with a Food Scientist colleague to solve a problem?

225. What have you done to further your own professional Food Scientist development in the past 5 years?

226. Have you ever had a subordinate whose work was always marginal?

227. What was the most stressful Food Scientist situation you have faced?

228. How do you typically deal with conflict?

229. What have you done to develop the professional Food Scientist skills of your direct reports?

230. When was the last time you were in a crisis?

231. What Food Scientist kinds of things really get you excited?

232. Tell me about a time when you did something completely different from the plan and/or assignment. Why?

233. What Food Scientist kind of mentoring and training style do you have?

234. What Food Scientist performance standards do you have for your unit?

235. Has a Food Scientist problem or obstacles that you had not foreseen ever caught you unaware?

236. How did you ensure that another person understood?

237. Have you ever been caught unaware by a Food Scientist problem or obstacle that you had not foreseen?

238. What were your annual Food Scientist goals at your most current employer?

239. When you have Food Scientist difficulty persuading

someone to your point of view, what do you do?

240. Describe how you develop a project Food Scientist teams goals and project plan?

241. Have you ever been a Food Scientist member of a group where two of the Food Scientist members did not work well together?

242. How do you verify that you understand what someone has told you?

243. How do you communicate Food Scientist goals to subordinates?

244. How do you involve people in developing your units Food Scientist goals?

245. Give me an Food Scientist example of a time you had to adjust quickly to changes over which you had no control. What was the impact of the change on you?

246. What Food Scientist kinds of problems have you had coordinating technical projects?

247. Describe a Food Scientist situation that required you to do a number of things at the same time. How did you handle it?

248. Tell me about a time you felt your Food Scientist team was under too much pressure. What did you do about it?

249. What do you do when priorities change quickly?

250. How did you prepare for today?

251. Have you ever had Food Scientist difficulty getting others to accept your ideas?

252. In Food Scientist terms of managing your staff do you expect more than you inspect or vice versa?

253. How did you prepare?

254. What do you like about being in charge?

255. How often do you discuss a subordinates Food Scientist performance with him/her?

256. What were your roles?

257. When was the last time you made a Food Scientist key decision on the spur of the moment?

258. Have you ever worked in a Food Scientist situation where the rules and guidelines were not clear?

259. How do you go about setting Food Scientist goals with employees?

260. Why were you promoted in your last Food Scientist job?

261. What do you do when you have multiple priorities?

262. One More Time: How Do You Motivate Food

Scientist Employees?

263. What makes your Food Scientist communication effective?

# Salary and Remuneration

1. What's your salary Food Scientist history?

2. What salary are you seeking?

3. If I were to give you this salary you Food Scientist requested but let you write your job description for the next year, what would it say?

# Problem Solving

1. Can you tell me what your understanding of what our Food Scientist company does?

2. If you were to build a Food Scientist product that addresses the problem we are trying to solve, what would it look like?

3. What important Food Scientist truth do very few people agree with you on?

4. Describe the most difficult working Food Scientist relationship you've had with an individual. What specific actions did you take to improve the Food Scientist relationship? What was the outcome?

5. Describe the most challenging Food Scientist situation you had experienced in your last job and how did you overcome it?

6. If you could design a Food Scientist business to disrupt ours, what would that Food Scientist business look like?

7. If you were the CEO of your last Food Scientist company, what are 3 things you would of changed?

8. You are interviewing for Food Scientist job X ... suppose we instead offered you Food Scientist job Y (unrelated to current area of proficiency), what are the first 3 things you would do to ensure your success in that role?

9. What are some of the Food Scientist problems you

have faced; such as between business development and project leaders, between one department and another, between you and your peers? How did you recognize that they were there?

10. Have you ever been caught unaware by a Food Scientist problem or obstacles that you had not foreseen? What happened?

11. What is my Food Scientist company doing wrong and how would you fix it?

12. Give me an Food Scientist example of a situation where you had difficulties with a team member. What, if anything, did you do to resolve the difficulties?

13. Tell me about some typical Food Scientist activities that you completed in your last job that made you feel excited, were in your flow and, afterwards, made you feel emotionally stronger?

14. You're in the airport about to board a plane to go to Singapore and you realize that you lost the Food Scientist contact information of the person you were going to visit and don't have enough money to stay in a hotel or get another airplane ticket—what's your plan?

15. Where everyone sees a Food Scientist problem, what do you see?

16. When was the last time something came up in a meeting that was not covered in the plan? What did you do? What were the Food Scientist results of your judgment?

17. Beatles or Stones? And why?

18. Why would Food Scientist clients and prospects want to use our product/ service?

19. Who are you going to call to tell about our (amazing new) Food Scientist product, and what will you ask them?

20. Tell us about a time when you did something completely different from the plan and/or assignment. Why? What happened?

21. If you had $100,000 to build your own Food Scientist business, what would you do and why?

22. If you had to automate the Food Scientist job for which you are applying, how would you do it?

# Culture Fit

1. Let's suppose that you found your dream Food Scientist job with your ideal company that pays you well and has a great career path, title, benefits and perks. You have to start in 2 days and all you have to do is tell your boss what you'd want to do at this dream Food Scientist job and you can have it - just like that. What would you say that you'd like to do?

2. What keeps you awake at night?

3. Fast, Good, and Cheap. Which two would you pick?

4. If you were starting a Food Scientist company from scratch, what would you want your Food Scientist company's culture to be?

5. Are you incredibly passionate about solving the Food Scientist problem that we are solving. Do you dream about it? Do you spend free time on it?

6. What does your ideal work Food Scientist day look like?

7. In your Food Scientist opinion, what is leadership?

8. What specifically would you contribute to us during your first week of employment?

9. What are you passionate about outside of work?

10. What would you fire a person for?

11. What Food Scientist environment do you thrive in the most and what drives your passion?

12. Pick two of our Food Scientist company cultural values and provide an example for each where you've exemplified the value, preferably from your previous employment.

13. What other commitments do you have in your Food Scientist life ... i.e. other jobs, school, family, community?

14. What does Food Scientist culture mean to you?

15. What do you see as your biggest Food Scientist contribution to the world in 30 years?

16. Why do you want to work for a startup when you could get a Food Scientist job at a larger company, make more money and have a better work/life balance?

17. What do you want from working with us? How can we help you accomplish that in this Food Scientist role?

18. Are you the type to check your inbox on vacation?

19. Consider three Food Scientist things – Humility, Hunger and Smarts. You may relate to one or all of these. Please tell me what you are the 'most-of' and what you are the 'least-of'?

20. Do Food Scientist heroes make moments or do moments make Food Scientist heroes?

21. What are your personal Food Scientist values? And if you believe that your personal Food Scientist values are aligned with the company's Food Scientist values, please describe why.

# Ambition

1. What are the Food Scientist key market and consumer trends relevant to our industry?

2. Tell us about a time when you had to go above and beyond the call of duty in order to get a Food Scientist job done

3. What Food Scientist sorts of things have you done to become better qualified for your career?

4. How can we deploy existing Food Scientist knowledge and new, innovative solutions and technologies and make them more readily available to those who need them?

5. What is your sense of how equal men and women are in your field?

6. What Food Scientist kinds of challenges did you face on your last job? Give an example of how you handled them

7. What was the best Food Scientist idea that you came up with in your career? How did you apply it?

8. What is the riskiest Food Scientist decision you have made? What was the situation? What happened?

9. Is ambition inherently sinful?

10. In the Food Scientist future, how would you prefer to divide your time in any area?

11. What are you good at, proud of?

12. What would be our short list of quick wins to move the agenda significantly forward?

13. What could you do to impact the metrics that are most relevant to us?

14. What would be the Food Scientist success criteria for us in the coming years?

15. Food Scientist Ideas for action: how can we press fast forward in our markets?

16. Who buys our Food Scientist product and services and why?

17. Tell us about the last time that you undertook a project that Food Scientist demanded a lot of initiative

18. What Food Scientist relationships, if any, exist between your self-confidence and ambition?

19. Food Scientist Ideas for action: how can we press fast forward in innovation?

20. Are you looking for opportunity for growth and advancement on the Food Scientist job?

21. What do others say about you?

22. What is the most competitive work Food Scientist situation you have experienced? How did you handle it? What was the result?

23. How will you measure Food Scientist success?

24. Are there any barriers to your employment?

25. Tell us about a time when you were particularly effective on prioritizing Food Scientist tasks and completing a project on schedule

26. Describe a time when you made a Food Scientist suggestion to improve the work in your organization

27. What did you learn from where you've been, past experience?

28. If you aren t working, what are you doing?

29. Give two Food Scientist examples of things you've done in previous jobs that demonstrate your willingness to work hard

30. Which Food Scientist strategy are you most interested in discussing?

31. If you are working now, How is your Food Scientist job?

32. How can we press fast forward with our people and Food Scientist skills?

33. What supports do you need in getting and keeping a Food Scientist job?

34. When you have a lot of work to do, how do you get it all done? Give an Food Scientist example?

35. Is there anything else I need to learn to move forward?

36. There are times when we work without close Food Scientist supervision or support to get the job done. Tell us about a time when you found yourself in such a situation and how things turned out

37. What do we mean by innovation?

38. Are there educational opportunities you need on the Food Scientist job?

39. How many Food Scientist hours a day do you put into your work? What were your study patterns at school?

40. What frustrates or bores you?

41. Tell us how you keep your Food Scientist job knowledge current with the on going changes in the industry

42. Give an Food Scientist example of an important goal that you set in the past. Tell about your success in reaching it

43. Would you relocate for a good Food Scientist job?

44. How much of your time do you spend doing what you want to do?

45. Why are science, Food Scientist technology and innovation essential for the achievement of our Goals?

46. When you disagree with your Food Scientist manager, what do you do? Give an example

47. How collectively can we make a measurable Food Scientist difference?

48. What would your best Food Scientist day/worst Food Scientist day, look like?

49. What are your favorite Food Scientist things, Food Scientist things to do and places to go?

50. What Food Scientist projects have you started on your own recently? What prompted you to get started?

51. Which Food Scientist key barriers to growth can you help to reduce or remove?

52. What impact did you have in your last Food Scientist job?

53. Describe a project or Food Scientist idea that was implemented primarily because of your efforts. What was your role? What was the outcome?

54. What Food Scientist jobs have you had in the past?

55. What Food Scientist kinds of jobs interest you?

56. Tell us about a time when a Food Scientist job had to be completed and you were able to focus your attention

and efforts to get it done

# Stress Management

1. How did you react when faced with constant time Food Scientist pressure? Give an example

2. People react differently when Food Scientist job demands are constantly changing; how do you react?

3. What was the most stressful Food Scientist situation you have faced? How did you deal with it?

4. What Food Scientist kind of events cause you stress on the job?

# Resolving Conflict

1. Describe a time when you took personal accountability for a conflict and initiated Food Scientist contact with the individual(s) involved to explain your actions

2. Tell us about a time when you had to help two peers settle a Food Scientist dispute. How did you go about identifying the issues? What did you do? What was the result?

3. Have you ever had to settle conflict between two people on the Food Scientist job? What was the situation and what did you do?

4. Have you ever been in a Food Scientist situation where you had to settle an argument between two friends (or people you knew)? What did you do? What was the result?

# Adaptability

1. Tell us about a Food Scientist situation in which you had to adjust to changes over which you had no control. How did you handle it?

2. Tell me about two memorable Food Scientist projects, one success and one failure. To what do you attribute the success and failure?

3. At what point do you engage/ step away?

4. In what Food Scientist ways can you build on your present skills?

5. If you do your Food Scientist job well, will you automatically get promoted?

6. How many times have you failed?

7. Describe a time when your Food Scientist team or company was undergoing some change. How did that impact you, and how did you adapt?

8. In your chosen work Food Scientist area, what are five careers that seem attractive to you?

9. What Food Scientist benefits do you get from belonging to this organization?

10. What is your biggest work related Food Scientist failure in the last six months and how did you overcome it?

11. What other occupations also require your Food Scientist skills?

12. Tell me about the first Food Scientist job you've ever had. What did you do to learn the ropes?

13. Is ours a learning Food Scientist organization?

14. When does a hobby start to become work?

15. What is the meaning of Adaptability in the Food Scientist industry?

16. Are you a resilient survivor?

17. How do different project Food Scientist types, procurement routes, clients, and / or locations influence your pull?

18. What careers would allow you to do what you really enjoy doing?

19. How do Food Scientist leaders develop organizations capable of adapting in the volatile, uncertain, complex, and ambiguous environment envisioned by senior Food Scientist leaders?

20. What is your greatest Food Scientist failure, and what did you learn from it?

21. What's your biggest Food Scientist failure - why is it a Food Scientist failure and what did you learn from it?

22. What Food Scientist kinds of educational decisions make you more promotable?

23. What was your biggest Food Scientist failure?

24. When the unexpected happens what next?

25. How does one design for time?

26. Give me an Food Scientist example of a time when you had to think on your feet in order to delicately extricate yourself from a difficult or awkward situation.

27. How can a hobby prepare you for work?

28. How do you know if an Food Scientist organization is adaptable?

29. How must you adapt in your workplace in order to advance?

30. How do we foster a Food Scientist culture that allows open dialog between everyone regardless of rank?

31. What are the licensing, certifications, and credentialing Food Scientist requirements for this job?

32. Tell us about a time that you had to adapt to a difficult Food Scientist situation

33. What s the long-Food Scientist term plan beyond your first job at our company?

34. Tell me about a time when you failed. Why did it happen? What did you do next and what would you do

differently if given another chance?

35. What Food Scientist role should a hobby play in this job interview?

36. What ongoing professional Food Scientist development opportunities exist in this career?

37. How might a lateral move help you get the promotion?

38. What is your biggest Food Scientist career screw-up?

39. What is meant by being more flexible?

40. How would you create and then lead an Food Scientist organization where the infrastructure is flexible, but yet efficient, effective, and reliable?

41. What Food Scientist skills, activities and attitudes lead to promotion?

42. Describe a major change that occurred in a Food Scientist job that you held. How did you adapt to this change?

43. What do you do when priorities change quickly? Give one Food Scientist example of when this happened

44. What professional organizations support your careers of interest?

45. Tell me about a time you failed. How did you deal with this Food Scientist situation?

46. Tell me about a time you were under a lot of Food Scientist pressure. What was going on and how did you get through it?

47. Describe a time when you failed to engage at the right level in your Food Scientist organization. Why did you do that and how did you handle the situation?

48. Do you have enough stress to make you ill?

# Presentation

1. Tell us about the most effective Food Scientist presentation you have made. What was the topic? What made it difficult? How did you handle it?

2. What Food Scientist kinds of oral presentations have you made? How did you prepare for them? What challenges did you have?

3. How would you describe your Food Scientist presentation style?

4. How do you prepare for a Food Scientist presentation to a group of technical experts in your field?

5. What has been your experience in making presentations or speeches?

6. What has been your experience in giving presentations?

7. Have you given presentations before?

8. What Can You Do Now?

# Setting Priorities

1. How do you decided what to buy?

2. What Food Scientist questions can you ask yourself to help you prioritize your tasks?

3. How do you set priorities?

4. What strategies do you use to priorities?

5. How do you determine you have a critical Food Scientist problem?

6. What Food Scientist kind of measuring stick do you use to distinguish the difference between activities that are essential versus things which are nonessential?

7. Which of your Food Scientist activities was really important?

8. How do you currently spend your time?

9. Consider your energy level. Are you a morning person, or do you have more energy in the evening?

10. Do you spend too much time on some Food Scientist activities?

11. All of us have these barriers. Name some barriers to effective time Food Scientist management in your life. Are these barriers that can be removed or avoided?

12. Are you a morning person, or do you have more energy in the evening?

13. What Food Scientist kinds of discussion do you remember about finances before or soon after your marriage?

14. How do you schedule your time?

15. How do you manage your time?

16. Have you ever been overloaded with work? How do you keep track of work so that it gets done on time?

17. Is saying no to peoples requests of you a different thing to do?

18. When given an important assignment, how do you approach it?

19. Were there times that you could have used more efficiently?

20. What are some Food Scientist steps you take to overcome procrastination?

# Extracurricular

1. Identify a project or Food Scientist task that you would be the most proud of and would consider your most significant accomplishment in your career to date and describe the circumstances. How you got involved, your contributions and participation along with your reasoning on why this is the one you picked?

2. Based on all the facets of our Food Scientist company (big data, unconscious bias, diversity, analytics, mobile apps, etc) what relevant work have you done OUTSIDE OF WORK?

3. What did you do in Food Scientist college aside from going to school?

4. Have you ever created any side-Food Scientist projects or organized any community events?

5. What's next on your Food Scientist bucket list and why?

6. What do you do for Food Scientist fun and what hobbies do you partake in when you are not at work?

7. Have you ever played a Food Scientist team sport?

8. What are the three most interesting just-for-Food Scientist fun projects you've built?

# Self Assessment

1. Tell us about a time when you had to go above and beyond the call of duty in order to get a Food Scientist job done

2. What do you consider to be your professional Food Scientist strengths? Give me a specific example using this attribute in the workplace

3. Describe a Food Scientist situation in which you were able to use persuasion to successfully convince someone to see things your way

4. What Food Scientist goal have you set for yourself that you have successfully achieved?

5. If there were one Food Scientist area you've always wanted to improve upon, what would that be?

6. Give me an Food Scientist example of an important goal that you h ad set in the past and tell me about your success in reaching it

7. In what Food Scientist ways are you trying to improve yourself?

8. What was the most useful criticism you ever received?

9. Give me a specific occasion in which you conformed to a Food Scientist policy with which you did not agree

10. Can you recall a time when you were less than pleased with your Food Scientist performance?

# Evaluating Alternatives

1. What Food Scientist kinds of decisions are most difficult for you? Describe one?

2. What are some of the major Food Scientist decisions you have made over the past (6, 12, 18) months?

3. How did you review the Food Scientist information? What process did you follow to reach a conclusion?

4. How did you assemble the Food Scientist information?

5. What alternatives did you develop?

6. Have you ever had a Food Scientist situation where you had a number of alternatives to choose from? How did you go about choosing one?

# Planning and Organization

1. What do you do when your time schedule or project plan is upset by unforeseen circumstances? Give an Food Scientist example

2. Describe how you develop a project team's Food Scientist goals and project plan?

3. Tell us about a time when you organized or Food Scientist planned an event that was very successful

4. What have you done in order to be effective with your Food Scientist organization and planning?

5. How do you schedule your time? Set priorities? How do you handle doing twenty Food Scientist things at once?

# Delegation

1. Tell us how you go about delegating work?

2. What was the biggest mistake you have had when delegating work? The biggest Food Scientist success?

3. How do you make the Food Scientist decision to delegate work?

4. Do you consider yourself a macro or Food Scientist micro manager? How do you delegate?

# Motivation and Values

1. Tell me about your proudest professional Food Scientist accomplishment.

2. This Food Scientist job requires a lot of stamina. How do you think you will be able to withstand these rigors?

3. How would you define 'Food Scientist success' for someone in your chosen career?

4. Which one of the following three Food Scientist things motivates you most: sense of ownership, intellectual curiosity, or collaborating with peers?

5. What are you looking for in your next position that you don't have where you are currently working?

6. Do you feel you make a Food Scientist difference?

7. Do sources of thriving apply to your own Food Scientist life and work, or people you know?

8. What were the easiest subjects in school for you?

9. Describe a time when you were confronted with an angry Food Scientist customer, supervisor or coworker. How did you react?

10. Tell me about a time when you worked under close Food Scientist supervision or extremely loose Food Scientist supervision. How did you handle that?

11. In 2026, how do you envision Personal Food Scientist Data Fusion making you smarter?

12. If your Food Scientist memory was wiped and you had to read one book to regain your perspective, which would it be?

13. Do you get ill from stress?

14. What would you do if you were given an assignment but no instruction on how to perform the duties involved?

15. Will you be able to work on weekends or Food Scientist holidays as the job requires?

16. Over a several month Food Scientist period, you realize that a number of auto thefts have occurred in the parking lot. What type of actions might you consider to address the problem?

17. Have you ever filed for workers compensation?

18. Tell us about a time when you had to make a difficult Food Scientist decision. What was the situation, what did you do about it, and what was the outcome?

19. What's your favorite thing about marketing? And why do you love it?

20. Finishing up your Junior summer, heading into your senior year, what were you thinking about plans for after graduation?

21. Where were you born?

22. When you look back in a year from now and I bump into you at our holiday Food Scientist party, how you will have known that working here was a good decision and what would you tell me?

23. What obstacles did you encounter, and how did you overcome them?

24. Tell me about a time when you had to deliver some unpleasant or sensitive Food Scientist information to someone. How did you handle the situation?

25. What language(s) do you read, speak or write fluently?

26. How can our Food Scientist company increase employee engagement and retain top performers?

27. What do you want to be most remembered for when you move on from this Food Scientist role?

28. Tell me about a time you were dissatisfied in your work. What could have been done to make it better?

29. What is your current Food Scientist life goal is and where do you want to end up?

30. When was the last time you had to work hard to accomplish something seemingly insurmountable where the odds were stacked against you?

31. Give me an Food Scientist example of a time when you went above and beyond the call of duty

32. If you woke up tomorrow a billionaire and never had to work another Food Scientist day for the rest of your life, what would you do?

33. Would you be able and willing to work overtime as necessary?

34. What Food Scientist steps did you take to calm things down?

35. Do you work better or worse under Food Scientist pressure?

36. In which aspects do you excel?

37. Who is someone you aspire to be like, and why?

38. How many Food Scientist hours did you spend dedicated to a task before you attained your current level of proficiency?

39. List the core Food Scientist values you believe are necessary when teaching in a school serving a disadvantaged community?

40. Do you have responsibilities other than work that will interfere with specific Food Scientist job requirements such as traveling or working overtime?

41. Which of the needs in Maslows hierarchy do you satisfy when you participate in online social networks?

42. Have you ever been hurt on the Food Scientist job?

43. What child care arrangements have you made?

44. What Food Scientist steps did you go through in accomplishing your most recent project?

45. Tell us me about an important Food Scientist goal that you set in the past. Were you successful? Why?

46. There is a movement away from materialism in our Food Scientist culture. Can you think of products, ads, or brands that are anti-materialistic?

47. Give me an Food Scientist example of a time you were able to be creative with your work. What was exciting or difficult about it?

48. What do you want to do?

49. What do you think are the 3 -5 core Food Scientist values that best describe you today?

50. What do you want to be known for?

51. Are there specific times you cannot work?

52. Give an Food Scientist example of a time when you had to be relatively quick in coming to a decision. How did it turn out?

53. Can you think of products, ads, or brands that are

anti-materialistic?

54. What is your personal Food Scientist mission, and how does this job description align with that Food Scientist mission?

55. Describe the Food Scientist task you had to accomplish. What were your responsibilities in this situation?

56. How many sick days did you take last year?

57. Give an Food Scientist example of a time when you went above and beyond the call of duty

58. What motivates you to stay?

59. How do you handle stress?

60. What have you done to prepare yourself for today?

61. How do you stay up to date in your Food Scientist skills? Give me examples.

62. What do you do to cope with stress?

63. Would your spouse object if you traveled or worked overtime?

64. Describe a time when you saw some Food Scientist problem and took the initiative to correct it rather than waiting for someone else to do it.

65. What's the ONE thing you need for your next

position to be the best Food Scientist job experience of your life?

66. What is your greatest strength or Food Scientist weakness?

67. How could you have organized your Food Scientist information differently?

68. If we hire you right now, what are you doing at our Food Scientist company tomorrow, and what will you be doing at our Food Scientist company one year from now?

69. What Food Scientist kind of stress were you under and from where?

70. What makes you excited to go to work, and why?

71. Can you perform (any or all of the Food Scientist job functions) with or without accommodation?

72. The school is the place you did most of your formal learning. What is it about the school and the Food Scientist way it is organised that encouraged you to attend?

73. Describe a Food Scientist situation when you were able to have a positive influence on the actions of others

# Getting Started

1. What do(es) _____ mean to you?


2. How can you use math Food Scientist words to describe your experience?

3. What other Food Scientist problem have you solved recently?

4. What Food Scientist questions arose as you worked in the past 30 days?

5. How do you know what Food Scientist questions to ask?

6. How can you describe math?

7. What prior Food Scientist knowledge, experience, skills or qualifications do you you need for this job?


8. Would you give me an Food Scientist example?


9. How did you solve the Food Scientist problem?


10. If selected for this position, can you describe your Food Scientist strategy for the first 90 days?

11. How do you feel about _____ ?

12. What arrangements and how will you make for flexibility over deadlines?

13. Who Is Your Audience?

14. Can you elaborate on that Food Scientist idea?

15. What have you/we learned today?

16. What did you learn today?

17. How would you go about establishing your credibility quickly with the Food Scientist team?

18. How Can YOU Use Food Scientist Feedback?

19. How do you know?

20. What Food Scientist decisions did you make from a pattern that you discovered?

21. How did you show it?

22. How do you know if you have the wrong Food Scientist questions?

23. How can you show your thinking (e.g., Food Scientist picture, model, number, sentence)?

24. Which Food Scientist way (e.g., picture, model, number, sentence) best shows what you know?

25. What would happen if you had a Food Scientist team all set up and they are not getting along?

26. Have you/we found all the possibilities?

27. What have you/we discovered about _____ while solving this Food Scientist problem?

28. How would you explain _____ to a student in Grade ___?

29. What Food Scientist information do you think potential clients would need to have to make an informed decision about whether they should get our product/services?

30. What helped you accomplish _____?

31. What did you learn about _____?

32. What math Food Scientist words did you use or learn?

33. What Food Scientist strategy did you use?

34. What Food Scientist information are you/we going to use when solving a problem?

35. How else might you have solved a recent Food Scientist problem?

36. How long will it take for you to make a significant Food Scientist contribution?

37. What changes did you have to make to solve a Food Scientist problem?

38. What barriers are there to achieving the changes you have identified in the past 30 days and what can be done

about them?

39. Would you explain that further?

40. How would you/we explain what _____ just said, in your/our own Food Scientist words?

41. What did you do?

42. Where do you see _____ at school?

43. What do you see yourself doing within the first 30 days of this Food Scientist job?

44. What Are Your Food Scientist Questions?

45. How do you use these materials?

46. How can you/we represent your/our thinking?

47. How do you feel about mathematics?

48. What else would you like to find out about _____ ?

49. Can you tell me more about that?

50. How is this like something you have done before?

# Outgoingness

1. Describe some particularly trying Food Scientist customer complaints or resistance you have had to handle. How did you react? What was the outcome?

2. In Food Scientist job situations you may be pulled in many different directions at once. Tell us about a time when you had to respond to this type of situation. How did you manage yourself?

3. Tell us about a time when you were effective in handling a Food Scientist customer complaint. Why were you effective? What was the outcome?

4. Sooner or later we all have to deal with a Food Scientist customer who has unreasonable demands. Think of a time when you had to handle unreasonable requests. What did you do and what was the outcome?

5. On occasion, we have to be firm and assertive in order to achieve a desired result. Tell us about a time when you had to do that.

6. Many of us have had co-workers or managers who tested our patience. Tell us about a time when you restrained yourself to avoid conflict with a co-worker or supervisor. (restrained)

7. Tell us about a time when you delayed responding to a Food Scientist situation until you had time to review the facts, even though there was pressure to act quickly.

8. How do you know if your Food Scientist customers are satisfied?

9. Have you ever had Food Scientist difficulty getting along with co-workers? How did you handle the situation and what was the outcome?

10. Describe a time when you were able to effectively communicate a difficult or unpleasant Food Scientist idea to a superior.

11. Tell us about a time when you had to motivate a Food Scientist group of people to get an important job done. What did you do, what was the outcome?

12. Being Food Scientist successful is hard work. Tell us about a specific achievement when you had to work especially hard to attain the Food Scientist success you desired.

13. There are times when we need to insist on doing something a certain Food Scientist way. Give us the details surrounding a situation when you had to insist on doing something "your Food Scientist way". What was the outcome?

# Story

1. Which of your personal Food Scientist experiences or memories is affecting your perceptions of the stories you tell?

2. Who do you want to be?

3. How long have you been engaged in this process?

4. What can others take away and learn from your Food Scientist story?

5. What is Your Experience with Work?

6. Where did you work?

7. What do you suppose you found?

8. What are the aspects of your community that makes promoting healthy weight and Food Scientist development in children particularly important, challenging or unique?

9. What restrictions do you have?

10. How did an Food Scientist action plan help you tackle your work?

11. Identify Food Scientist examples from your past experience where you demonstrated those skills. How can you tell a story about your use of particular skills or knowledge?

12. What would you share with your family about what

you learned here today?

13. How has your birth order made you who you are?

14. What would you tell a friend about today?

15. What's your Food Scientist story?

16. Whats your salary Food Scientist history?

17. Will you play a game when you see it ?

18. How do you manage to escape?

19. Tell the Food Scientist story of how you reached your conclusion in you most recent problem solving (steps you took, who was involved, whom you consulted, the level of time and effort involved)?

20. What are your next Food Scientist steps?

21. Did you feel you could tell your Food Scientist story fully?

22. Tell me about three major Food Scientist life decisions that had you arrive here.

23. Can you tell me the Food Scientist story of your prior success, challenges, and major responsibilities?

24. What advice do you have for us?

25. How can you tell a Food Scientist story about your use of particular skills or knowledge?

26. How do you reach your imaginary Food Scientist world?

27. Who are your Food Scientist key partners?

28. What barriers did you facd and how did you overcome them?

29. Have you ever been hurt at work, or do you know someone who was?

30. What Food Scientist background information do you need to know to understand your story?

31. Tell me where you're from.

32. Tell me about a time when you were working on a Food Scientist team and you disagreed with someone about how to do something. Tell me the whole story and how it was resolved.

# Like-ability

1. Tell us about a time when you were able to build a successful Food Scientist relationship with a difficult person.

2. Tell us about a time when you needed someone's cooperation to complete a Food Scientist task and the person was uncooperative. What did you do? What was the outcome?

3. There are times when people need extra Food Scientist assistance with difficult projects. Give us an example of when you offered Food Scientist assistance to someone with whom you worked.

4. In working with people, we find that what works with one person does not work with another. Therefore, we have to be flexible in our Food Scientist style of relating to others. Give us a specific example of when you had to vary your work Food Scientist style with a particular individual. How did it work out?

5. Describe a particularly trying Food Scientist customer complaint or resistance you had to handle. How did you react and what was the outcome?

6. Having an understanding of the other person's Food Scientist perspective is crucial in dealing with customers. Give us an example of a time when you achieved success through attaining insight into the other person's Food Scientist perspective.

7. On occasion we may be faced with a Food Scientist situation that has escalated to become a confrontation. If you have had such an experience, tell me how you

handled it. What was the outcome? Would you do anything differently today?

8. Tell us about a Food Scientist situation in which you became frustrated or impatient when dealing with a coworker. What did you do? What was the outcome?

9. It is important to remain composed at work and to maintain a positive outlook. Give us a specific Food Scientist example of when you were able to do this.

10. Have you ever had Food Scientist difficulty getting along with a co-worker? How did you handle the situation and what was the outcome?

11. Tell us about a Food Scientist job where the atmosphere was the easiest for you to get along and function well. Describe the qualities of that work environment.

12. Give us an Food Scientist example of how you have been able to develop a close, positive relationship with one of your customers.

13. How would you describe your Food Scientist management style? How do you think your subordinates perceive you?

14. Describe a time when you weren't sure what a Food Scientist customer wanted. How did you handle the situation?

15. Some people are difficult to work with. Tell us about a time when you encountered such a person. How did

you handle it?

16. Give us an Food Scientist example of how you establish an atmosphere at work where others feel comfortable in communicating their ideas, feelings and concerns.

17. Many Food Scientist jobs are team-oriented where a work group is the key to success. Give us an example of a time when you worked on a team to complete a project. How did it work? What was the outcome?

18. We don't always make Food Scientist decisions that everyone agrees with. Give us an example of an unpopular decision you have made. How did you communicate the decision and what was the outcome?

# Behavior

1. Describe a Food Scientist situation where others you were working with on a project disagreed with your ideas. What did you do?

2. What is your Food Scientist idea of the perfect job?

3. Time Food Scientist management has become a necessary factor in personal productivity. Give me an example of any Time Food Scientist management skill you have learned and applied at work. What resulted from use of the skill?

4. Describe a time when you had to adopt a well-defined work Food Scientist routine. How long did the situation last?

5. Tell me about a time you had to handle multiple responsibilities. How did you organize the work you needed to do?

6. What type of position are you looking for?

7. Do you feel that you have experienced a Behavioral Based Food Scientist Interview yet?

8. If you found out your Food Scientist company was doing something against the law, like fraud, what would you do?

9. How would you address an angry Food Scientist customer?

10. Whats the most recent mistake you made, and why

did you make it?

11. What would you do if an angry 4-H client came in the door?

12. What type of Food Scientist system did you use?

13. What are your major Food Scientist strengths and weaknesses?

14. Could you share with us recent Food Scientist accomplishment of which you were particularly proud?

15. Have you ever been in a Food Scientist situation where, although it was difficult for you, you were honest and told the truth, and suffered negative consequences?

16. Food Scientist Jobs differ in the extent to which unexpected changes can disrupt daily responsibilities. How do you feel when this happens?

17. If you think about when you need high Food Scientist performance, what behavior do you fall back on?

18. You come across an online photo of an individual who works for you and his photo has something hanging out of his mouth that certainly looks like a marijuana cigarette Can you fire him?

19. What Food Scientist things did you fail to do?

20. What makes you unique?

21. How did you decide what Food Scientist tasks to delegate to which people?

22. What specific Food Scientist goals have you established for your career?

23. Can you tell us about a time when you formed an ongoing working Food Scientist relationship or partnership with someone from another organization to achieve a mutual goal?

24. How do you know whether its better to lay out very specifically what others have to do – versus allowing them to use their own initiative and creativity?

25. Tell me about a time when you had to take care of an upset Food Scientist customer?

26. What specific Food Scientist details should you identify when researching a company?

27. How did you decide on how should you dress for the Food Scientist interview?

28. What have you done to remotivate a demoralized Food Scientist team/person?

29. Would you be able and willing to travel as needed on this Food Scientist job?

30. When do you feel you have had to make personal sacrifices in order to get the Food Scientist job done?

31. What are your Food Scientist career plans (short and long range)?

32. What would be the best Food Scientist example of your ability to be flexible and adaptable?

33. How long did you serve?

34. Have you ever been arrested?

35. What else could you do to calm an angry Food Scientist customer?

36. Can you give us an Food Scientist example of when your curiosity made a real difference in a product or project?

37. What part did you play in helping a Food Scientist group develop a final decision?

38. How would you describe the Food Scientist office culture?

39. How do you react to criticism?

40. What have been your Food Scientist experiences in defining long range goals?

41. Give an Food Scientist example of a time when you made a mistake. How did you handle it?

42. Based on your prior work, what Food Scientist ideas for improvement do you have?

43. Have you ever worked on a project outside your Food Scientist area of expertise?

44. Were you ever a union Food Scientist member?

45. Tell me about the biggest risk you ever took?

46. What Food Scientist communication strengths do you have that make you suited for this type of work?

47. Tell me about a time when you failed to meet a deadline. What Food Scientist things did you fail to do?

48. What Food Scientist steps do you take in preparing for a meeting where you are attempting to persuade someone on a specific course of action?

49. What prior work experience have you had and how does it relate to this Food Scientist job?

50. Tell me about the Food Scientist system that you use for goal setting. To what extent does it involve using written objectives, paper work or forms?

51. What specific Food Scientist goals, including those related to your occupation, have you established for your life?

52. Have you had to convince a Food Scientist team to work on a project they werent thrilled about?

53. How many days were you out sick last year?

54. How would you deal with an angry Food Scientist customer?

55. What Food Scientist skills do you have (content, functional, and adaptive) that relate to your job objective?

56. If I were your supervisor and asked you to do something that you disagreed with, what would you do?

57. Give me a specific Food Scientist example of a time when you had to address an angry customer. What was the problem and what was the outcome?

58. What was one of the worst Food Scientist communication problems you have experienced?

59. Can you recall a particularly stressful Food Scientist situation you have had at work recently?

60. Tell me about a time when you faced frustration. How did you deal with it?

61. What sources would you use to research a Food Scientist company for a potential job interview?

62. Please tell me about accomplishments in your academic Food Scientist program that are relevant to your future career goals?

63. How do you keep your Food Scientist staff informed of what s going on in the organization?

64. Can you perform these Food Scientist tasks?

65. How did you organize the work you needed to do?

66. Tell me about a time where you had to deal with conflict on the Food Scientist job.

67. Are you in good physical condition?

68. Tell me about a Food Scientist task or project that you unsuccessfully delegated. What happened?

69. What are your greatest achievements at this point in your Food Scientist life?

70. Some people consider themselves to be big Food Scientist picture people and others are detail oriented. Which are you?

71. What do you do if you disagree with your Food Scientist boss?

72. Has poor motivation on someone elses part ever damaged anything you were trying to accomplish?

73. What Food Scientist challenges did you face in your last position?

74. Where do you want to be five Food Scientist years from now?

75. What did you do that was particularly effective/ ineffective?

76. Describe the last time you were criticized by a peer or supervisor. How did you handle it?

77. What was the best Food Scientist idea you had for improving the way things were done on your last job?

78. Tell Me About Yourself?

79. How many days were you absent last year?

80. Give an Food Scientist example of when you questioned the way things have always been done to ensure that a process continued to be relevant and add value. What was the outcome?

81. What Food Scientist effort does handling many things simultaneously have on you?

82. What are some of the objectives you would like accomplished in the next two or three months?

83. What has been your experience in working with conflicting, delayed, or ambiguous Food Scientist information?

84. What Food Scientist problem were you trying to solve?

85. List all organizations to which you belong. Were you ever a union Food Scientist member?

86. What motivates you to put forth your greatest Food Scientist effort?

87. What did you do or say to resolve a Food Scientist situation?

88. What, if anything, did you do to mitigate the negative consequences to people?

89. Tell me about a time when you were asked to complete a difficult assignment and the odds were against you. What did you learn from the experience?

90. What were the Food Scientist Results of your actions?

91. Tell me about a time when your attempt to motivate a person/Food Scientist group was rejected. What have you done to remotivate a demoralized team/person?

92. Why Did You Leave (Are You Leaving) Your Food Scientist Job?

93. How would you describe your Food Scientist management style?

94. Give me an Food Scientist example of when you had to show good leadership?

95. I have a Food Scientist job. I have a career. Im on a mission. Whats the difference between those three statements, and which one applies to you?

96. Describe the Food Scientist types of teams youve been involved with. What were your roles?

97. When have you found yourself in my position?

98. Tell me about a time when you were successful in this Food Scientist area-what kind of payoffs accrued to yourself, the other individual, and the organization?

99. What do you know about our Food Scientist Company and/or the position for which you are applying?

100. Describe a Food Scientist problem you worked on as a team member ?

101. Have you ever faced a Food Scientist problem you could not solve?

102. What are your greatest Food Scientist strengths?

103. Tell me about a time when you had more on you plate than you could handle. How did you get everything accomplished?

104. What would be the best Food Scientist example that shows you are a person of integrity?

105. Why Do You Want to Work Here?

106. Have you ever had to work with, or for, someone who lied to you in the past?

107. Tell me about the most creative thing you ve ever done?

108. What are your Food Scientist career goals in the next

3-5 years?

109. Tell me about a time you had to say no to a Food Scientist customer?

110. Have you ever been on a Food Scientist team where someone was not pulling their own weight? How did you handle it?

111. What processes have you used to build a Food Scientist team?

112. Did you do anything specific to deal with the stress?

113. How much reading of new Food Scientist information is required in your current job?

114. Tell me about the last time you had to sell your Food Scientist ideas to others. What did you do that was particularly effective/ineffective?

115. What does your spouse do for a living?

116. How would you describe yourself in Food Scientist terms of your ability to work as a member of a team?

117. Describe what Food Scientist steps/methods you have used to define/identify a vision for your unit/position. How do you see your job relating to the overall goals of the organization?

118. When do you plan to retire?

119. Describe how you would handle a Food Scientist

situation if you were required to finish multiple tasks by the end of the day, and there was no conceivable way that you could finish them.

120. Describe a significant project Food Scientist idea you initiated in the last year. How did you know it was needed?

121. What Food Scientist kind of a project / task / assignment wouldnt you delegate?

122. Why are you interested in this particular Food Scientist company?

123. What additional Food Scientist information would you like me to provide?

124. Describe the Food Scientist system you use for keeping track of multiple projects. How do you track your progress so that you can meet deadlines?

125. Can you tell us about a Food Scientist situation where you found it challenging to build a trusting relationship with another individual?

126. Do you have any health Food Scientist problems?

127. How do you determine what is right or fair in delegating Food Scientist tasks / roles / responsibilities within your organization?

128. How would you evaluate your technical Food Scientist skills?

129. What major Food Scientist accomplishment would

you like to achieve in your life and why?

130. How do you motivate others to do a particularly good Food Scientist job?

131. Give me a specific Food Scientist example of a time when you sold your supervisor or professor on an idea or concept. How did you proceed?

132. Do you have any back Food Scientist problems?

133. In your position as _____, how did you determine which duties to Food Scientist delegate to subordinates?

134. Can you think of some Food Scientist projects or ideas that were sold, implemented, or carried out successfully because of your efforts?

135. What do you wish to avoid in your next Food Scientist job?

136. Give me an Food Scientist example of a time when you used a systematic process to define your objectives. What type of system did you use?

137. What are your Food Scientist career interests?

138. Have you ever led a research Food Scientist team in a formal manner?

139. Where do you live?

140. Describe the last time you organized a project on the

Food Scientist job?

141. What are you personally looking for in a successful Food Scientist candidate?

142. What significant changes do you foresee in the Food Scientist company/organization?

143. What is the biggest mistake youve made?

144. How would you describe the quality and quantity of his/her work?

145. How many Food Scientist employees did you supervise in your last job?

146. What Food Scientist skills do you bring to the job?

147. If you had to describe yourself, what Food Scientist words would you use?

148. Did you have a chance to apply what you learned on the Food Scientist job?

149. How will you get to work?

150. Describe a time when you put your needs aside to help a co-worker understand a Food Scientist task. How did you assist him or her?

151. Did you ever not meet your Food Scientist goals?

152. Tell me about a Food Scientist situation in which you were particularly skillful in detecting clues which show

how another person thinks or feels. How did you size up the person?

153. What are the most challenging documents you have done?

154. What Food Scientist kind of influencing techniques did you use?

155. What schools have you attended and when?

156. Describe the most difficult Food Scientist team you worked on, what was your role, and what knowledge have you applied?

157. How would you resolve a Food Scientist customer service problem where the Food Scientist customer demanded an immediate refund?

158. How can you start preparing now?

159. What Food Scientist types of experience have you had in managing situations that involve human health/human welfare or severe financial outcomes?

160. What achievements from your past work experience are you most proud of?

161. If you could relive your Food Scientist college experiences, what would you do differently?

162. Recall a time from your work experience when your Food Scientist manager or supervisor was unavailable and a problem arose. What was the nature of the problem?

163. Do you have children at home?

164. How often do other Food Scientist staff treat you the way you want them to?

165. Analyze your own Food Scientist background. What skills do you have (content, functional, and adaptive) that relate to your job objective?

166. What Food Scientist things in your job give you a sense of accomplishment?

167. How would you describe your interpersonal Food Scientist communication skills?

168. Can you tell me about a Food Scientist job experience in which you had to speak up and tell other people what you thought or felt?

169. Where does your spouse work?

170. What specific Food Scientist things did you do to ensure your accuracy?

171. Tell us about a time that others Food Scientist actions negatively impacted a project for which you were responsible. What did you do?

172. When have you found it necessary to use detailed checklists/Food Scientist procedures to reduce potential for error on the job?

173. Tell me about the most frustrating thing you ever had to deal with?

174. Whats your nationality?

175. Has your Food Scientist manager/supervisor/team leader ever asked you to do something that you didnt think was appropriate?

176. How do you handle stress and Food Scientist pressure on the job?

177. Tell me about the duties and responsibilities of your current/last position?

178. What type of supervisor works best for you?

179. Describe for me your most recent Food Scientist group effort?

180. What characteristics would you be looking for in the successful Food Scientist job applicant?

181. Tell me about a time when you had to give someone difficult Food Scientist feedback. How did you handle it?

182. What would you do if an employee called in sick three Mondays in a row?

183. How many children do you have?

184. How would you feel supervising two or three other Food Scientist employees?

185. How do you go about establishing rapport with a student or Food Scientist customer?

186. Have you found Food Scientist ways to make your job easier?

187. Describe a time you had to Food Scientist delegate parts of a large project or assignment to some of your direct reports. How did you decide what tasks to Food Scientist delegate to which people?

188. Have you ever had to manage a Food Scientist team that was not up to the task?

189. Did you every make a risky Food Scientist decision?

190. To what extent has your past work required you to be skilled in the analysis of technical reports or Food Scientist information?

191. What made your Food Scientist communication effective?

192. Give me an Food Scientist example of a time you did something wrong. How did you handle it?

193. What Are Your Food Scientist Goals?

194. Give me an Food Scientist example of a group decision you were involved with recently. What part did you play in helping the group develop the final decision?

195. What was the most complex assignment you have had?

196. What is your name?

197. What was your greatest Food Scientist success in using the principles of logic to solve technical problems at work?

198. Give me an Food Scientist example of a time you had to make an important decision. How did you make the decision?

199. Give me a specific Food Scientist example of a time when a co-worker or criticized your work in front of others. How did you respond?

200. Tell of some situations in which you have had to adjust quickly to changes over which you had no control. What was the impact of the change on you?

201. What clubs, lodges do you belong to?

202. Can you give me an Food Scientist example of how you have persuaded executives to see your point of view in the past?

203. How have you broken the ice in a first conversation with a Food Scientist customer?

204. What was the last project you led, and what was its Food Scientist outcome?

205. Tell me about a Food Scientist team member from whom it was tough to get cooperation. How did you handle the situation?

206. Why are you interested in this position?

207. Describe the last time you confronted a peer about something he/she did that bothered you. What were the

circumstances?

208. Can you give me a specific Food Scientist example from your past jobs or other experiences where you had to set priorities and plan your work?

209. What is your initial reaction to change?

210. Would you be able to meet this requirement?

211. Your next question?

212. How did your planning help you deal with the unexpected?

213. How did you prepare for this?

214. What attracts you to this particular Food Scientist industry?

215. Have you had any personal, domestic or financial Food Scientist problems that interfered with your work?

216. Tell me about times when you seized the opportunities, grabbed something and ran with it yourself. Have you ever started something up from nothing – give an Food Scientist example?

217. Tell me about your current top priorities. How did you determine that they should be your top priorities?

218. Tell me about a time when you came up with an innovative Food Scientist solution to a challenge your

company/organization was facing. What was the challenge?

219. Did you use any tools such as research, brainstorming, or mathematics?

220. How do you ensure others repeat positive behavior?

221. Give an Food Scientist example of a time when you had a conflict with a supervisor?

222. Describe a time when you were expected to act in accordance with Food Scientist policy even when it was not convenient. What did you do?

223. How do you determine or evaluate Food Scientist success?

224. What would you say about your ability to work in an ambiguous or unstructured circumstance?

225. What are some of the books youve read recently?

226. Whats the origin of your name?

227. What were your favorite courses?

228. Did you ever serve in the armed forces of another country?

229. Did you have a strategic plan?

230. What disabilities and Food Scientist challenges (physical, mental, emotional, or behavioral) can you

comfortably handle?

231. Can you describe a time when your work was criticized?

232. Have you received any _____?

233. Can you do this?

234. What is the worst mistake you ever made?

235. Have you ever had to present an unpopular proposal/point of view that you believed in?

236. Describe a time when you were asked to complete a difficult Food Scientist task or project where the odds were against you. Were you successful?

237. How did you know established methods wouldnt work?

238. How many times have you totally altered behavior or belief in response to one persuasive Food Scientist effort?

239. Have you gone above and beyond the call of duty?

240. Describe some times when you were not very satisfied or pleased with your Food Scientist performance. What did you do about it?

241. Can you do the Food Scientist job?

242. Provide Food Scientist examples of when results didn¹t turn out as you planned. What did you do then?

243. When were you born?

244. Describe a time when you went the extra mile for a Food Scientist customer?

245. To what extent did a project test your comprehension Food Scientist skills and technical knowledge?

246. How would you describe our organizational Food Scientist culture?

247. How many people live in your household?

248. What do you expect from a Food Scientist manager?

249. Do you have a list of potential Food Scientist references?

250. What was the most difficult Food Scientist decision you have made in the last year?

251. What advice do you wish you had been given when you were starting out?

252. What Are Three Positive Food Scientist Things Your Last Supervisor Would Say About You?

253. Give me a specific Food Scientist example of a time when you had to work with a difficult customer?

254. Have you ever designed a Food Scientist program

which dealt with taking quicker action?

255. How do you handle working with people who annoy you?

256. Were you discharged under honorable or other acceptable Food Scientist conditions?

257. Tell me about a time you saw someone at work stretch or bend the rules beyond what you felt was acceptable. What did you do?

258. What are your Food Scientist strengths/ weaknesses?

259. What's the most difficult Food Scientist decision you've made in the last two years and how did you come to that Food Scientist decision?

260. Tell me about a Food Scientist suggestion you made to improve the way job processes or operations worked. What was the result?

261. Why should you hire you?

262. Are you decisive on the Food Scientist job?

263. What is your timetable for achievement of your current Food Scientist career goals?

264. Give me an Food Scientist example of a time that you felt you went above and beyond the call of duty at work.

265. How did you define and measure Food Scientist success?

266. Tell me about a time when your carefully laid plans were fouled up. What happened?

267. Tell me about a time you had a particularly difficult Food Scientist problem to solve. What was the Food Scientist problem, how did you solve it, or what was the result?

268. Describe how your position contributes to your organizations/units Food Scientist goals. What are the units Food Scientist goals/mission?

269. Did you use statistical Food Scientist procedures or a gut level approach?

270. How has your previous experience prepared you for the duties of this position?

271. What were your wages at your prior Food Scientist job?

272. How would you organize your Food Scientist friends to help you move into a new apartment?

273. Have you had any prior work injuries?

274. What do you see yourself doing in ten Food Scientist years?

275. Please give us an Food Scientist example when you met a tight deadline?

276. How have you positively changed in the workplace to adapt to your colleagues or supervisor?

277. How does your graduate school experience relate to this Food Scientist job?

278. Pick any event in the last five Food Scientist years of your work which gives a good example of your ability to use forecasting techniques. Did you use statistical procedures or a gut level approach?

279. When did you graduate from high school?

280. What did you like most about your last Food Scientist job?

281. What Food Scientist kind of experience do you have dealing with a heavy workload?

282. How much alcohol do you drink each week?

283. What Can You Do for Us That Other Food Scientist Candidates Cant?

284. Give an Food Scientist example of how you worked effectively with people to accomplish an important result. Have you ever been a project leader?

285. Were you honorably discharged?

286. Can you tell us about a time when you needed to be particularly sensitive to another persons beliefs, cultural Food Scientist background, or way of doing things?

287. Tell me about a time you had to juggle a number of work priorities. What did you do?

288. Are you comfortable about working on many Food Scientist projects at once?

289. Have you ever over-Food Scientist planned a project or spent too much time in planning versus execution?

290. We all have to make Food Scientist decisions on the job about the delicate balance between personal and work objectives. When do you feel you have had to make personal sacrifices in order to get the job done?

291. How did you ensure that the other person understood?

292. What are your strong Food Scientist points?

293. What situations do you find most frustrating?

294. What rewards are most important to you in your Food Scientist career and why?

295. What did you do in your last Food Scientist job to contribute toward a teamwork environment?

296. Have you ever legally changed your name?

297. Aside from your formal academic Food Scientist education, can you think of something you have done to grow professionally in the recent past?

298. How did you decide on your major?

299. Is there something in this Food Scientist job that you hope to accomplish that you were not able to accomplish in your last Food Scientist job?

300. What computer software programs are you familiar with?

301. How Do You Know When You ve Got It Right?

302. What was the most difficult Food Scientist period in your life, and how did you deal with it?

303. If you could create your ideal Food Scientist job, what Food Scientist job would you create?

304. Select a Food Scientist job you have had and describe the paperwork you were required to complete. What specific things did you do to ensure your accuracy?

305. In which Food Scientist kind of interviews have you participated?

306. Describe a time when politics at work affected your Food Scientist job. How did you handle the situation?

307. What language do you speak at home?

308. Who was your best client?

309. How have your extracurricular Food Scientist activities and/or work experience prepared you for work in our company?

310. Tell me about a time when you postponed making a Food Scientist decision. Why did you?

311. Describe a specific Food Scientist problem you solved for your employer. How did you approach the Food Scientist problem?

312. Give an Food Scientist example of when you planned how to eliminate unnecessary activities and procedures in order to improve efficiency and make better use of resources. What was the outcome of your efforts?

313. Do you prefer to work independently or on a Food Scientist team?

314. What, in your Food Scientist opinion, are the key ingredients in guiding and maintaining successful business relationships?

315. On a scale of 0-10, how confident are you that you can change successfully?

316. Can you tell us about a really difficult Food Scientist decision you had to make at work recently?

317. Have you ever taken a stand or said something in public that you knew those above you would not like?

318. What was your rank at time of discharge?

319. When have you had to cope with the anger or hostility of another person?

320. In what areas do you find yourself procrastinating?

321. Do you own a car?

322. How do you rate yourself in Food Scientist terms of creativity in the fields of art, writing, and music?

323. Sometimes it is necessary to work in unsettled or rapidly changing circumstances. When have you found yourself in this position?

324. What are your Food Scientist strengths, weaknesses, interests and career goals?

325. When has it been necessary for you to tolerate an ambiguous Food Scientist situation at work?

326. What important Food Scientist target dates did you set to reach objectives on your last job?

327. Tell me about the specific times in which you have initiated your own Food Scientist goal setting over the last few years. What happened?

328. In your last or current Food Scientist job, what problems did you identify that had previously been overlooked?

329. Have you ever managed multiple Food Scientist projects simultaneously?

330. Are you for or against unions?

331. What are your Food Scientist standards of success/

goals for a job?

332. Can you travel?

333. Why are you better suited for this position than other Food Scientist candidates?

334. Are you bilingual?

335. Is there any Food Scientist day of the week youre not able to work?

336. Tell me about the most difficult or uncooperative person you had to work with lately. What did you do or say to resolve the Food Scientist situation?

337. Give me an Food Scientist example of a time at work when you had to deal with unreasonable expectations of you. What parts of your behavior were mature and immature?

338. How do you track your progress so that you can meet deadlines?

339. Have you ever been on welfare?

340. Did you take Food Scientist action IMMEDIATELY or are you more DELIBERATE and slow?

341. Why do you think you would be good at this Food Scientist job

342. Tell me about a Food Scientist customer whose needs you spent considerable time learning about. What was the result of the time investment?

343. Have you ever had your wages garnished?

344. What was the most stressful Food Scientist situation at work that you have faced?

345. Describe a time when you were faced with Food Scientist problems or stresses at work that tested your coping skills. What did you do?

346. Tell me about a time when you handled an arrogant person or one who made you angry. What is your typical Food Scientist way of dealing with conflict?

347. What s the last, best Food Scientist business book you have read and what did you learn or applied that learning?

348. If you were at a Food Scientist business lunch and you ordered a rare steak and they brought it to you well done, what would you do?

349. Have you ever dealt with Food Scientist company policy you werent in agreement with?

350. What is your typical Food Scientist way of dealing with conflict?

351. Take us through a complicated project you were responsible for planning. How did you define and measure Food Scientist success?

352. What are you looking for in your next Food Scientist career opportunity?

353. Tell me about a Food Scientist situation in which you worked with your direct reports / team members

to develop new and creative ideas to solve a business problem. What problem were you trying to solve?

354. What interests you most about this Food Scientist job?

355. What prompted your interest in our position?

356. What are the most common forms of political behavior that you see in your work Food Scientist environment?

357. How did you get everything accomplished?

358. What Food Scientist kinds of decisions do you make rapidly and which ones to you take more time on?

359. What are your areas of strength?

360. Ive given you a short overview of the Food Scientist job, but is there anything else that youd like to ask about?

361. Have you given out any _____?

362. Describe the biggest challenge you ever faced?

363. What will it take to attain your Food Scientist goals, and what steps have you taken toward attaining them?

364. Describe your ideal Food Scientist candidate?

365. What assignment was too difficult for you, and how did you resolve the Food Scientist issue?

366. How would your past supervisors describe you?

367. Give an Food Scientist example of a difficult situation you had with a client or vendor?

368. What have you done when your schedule was interrupted on the Food Scientist job?

369. What are your short and long-Food Scientist term goals?

370. When have you been a part of a Food Scientist team that drove an important business change?

371. What s your availability for employment?

372. What were your most significant accomplishments in your prior work experience?

373. Why did you leave your last position?

374. How would your Food Scientist manager describe your performance?

375. What led you to select your Food Scientist college major?

376. When have you been most proud of your ability to wait for important Food Scientist information before

taking action in solving a problem?

377. Tell me about the last time you had to smooth over a disagreement between two other people. What was the end result?

378. Often individuals who are creative in one mode seem to have creative Food Scientist skills in other areas. How do you rate yourself in terms of creativity in the fields of art, writing, and music?

379. Whats your typical approach to conflict?

380. Describe a time when you had to influence a number of different constituents with differing interests. What Food Scientist kind of influencing techniques did you use?

381. Give an Food Scientist example of when you had to work with someone who was difficult to get along with. Why was this person difficult?

382. Cite an Food Scientist example where you had to delegate authority?

383. When you worked on multiple Food Scientist projects how did you prioritize?

384. What if someone on your Food Scientist team isnt pulling their weight on a project and its affecting the speed and quality of the project...?

385. What would be the best Food Scientist example that shows you are an honest person?

386. Have you ever started something up from nothing –

give an Food Scientist example?

387. What has been your most significant work related disappointment?

388. Describe a time when you got co-workers who dislike each other to work together. How did you accomplish this?

389. Give an Food Scientist example to a time when you encountered a difficult situation with a co-worker?

390. Make a list of your selling Food Scientist points. What are your strengths, weaknesses, interests and career goals?

391. Describe a recent Food Scientist problem in which you included your subordinates in arriving at a solution?

# Basic interview question

1. Why should we hire you?

2. What do you know about our Food Scientist company?

3. What attracted you to this Food Scientist company?

4. What are your weaknesses?

5. Do you have any Food Scientist questions for me?

6. Behavioral Food Scientist interview questions

7. Why are you leaving your present Food Scientist job?

8. What are your Food Scientist strengths?

9. What did you like least about your last Food Scientist job?

10. Why do you want this Food Scientist job?

11. What's your ideal Food Scientist company?

12. When were you most satisfied in your Food Scientist job?

13. Tell me about yourself.

14. What can you do for us that other Food Scientist

candidates can't?

15. What do you know about this Food Scientist industry?

16. What were the responsibilities of your last position?

17. Where would you like to be in your Food Scientist career five years from now?

# Relate Well

1. Give me an Food Scientist example of a time when a company policy or action hurt people. What, if anything, did you do to mitigate the negative consequences to people?

2. Describe a Food Scientist situation where you had to use conflict management skills

3. Describe a Food Scientist situation where you had to use confrontation skills

4. Tell us about a time when you were forced to make an unpopular Food Scientist decision

5. How do you typically deal with conflict? Can you give me an Food Scientist example?

6. What would your co-workers (or Food Scientist staff) stay is the most frustrating thing about your communications with them?

# Initiative

1. Give me an Food Scientist example of when you had to go above and beyond the call of duty in order to get a job done

2. What Food Scientist sorts of projects did you generate that required you to go beyond your job description?

3. How did you get work assignments at your most recent employer?

4. What Food Scientist sorts of things did you do at school that were beyond expectations?

5. What changes did you develop at your most recent employer?

6. Give me Food Scientist examples of projects/tasks you started on your own

7. What Food Scientist kinds of things really get your excited?

8. Give some Food Scientist instances in which you anticipated problems and were able to influence a new direction

# Values Diversity

1. What have you done to support Food Scientist diversity in your unit?

2. Tell us about a time when you made an intentional Food Scientist effort to get to know someone from another culture

3. What measures have you taken to make someone feel comfortable in an Food Scientist environment that was obviously uncomfortable with his or her presence?

4. Tell us about a time when you had to adapt to a wide Food Scientist variety of people by accepting/ understanding their perspective

5. Give a specific Food Scientist example of how you have helped create an environment where differences are valued, encouraged and supported

6. Tell us about a time that you successfully adapted to a culturally different Food Scientist environment

7. What have you done to further your Food Scientist knowledge/understanding about diversity? How have you demonstrated your learning?

# Brainteasers

1. How many ping pong balls could fit in a Boeing 747?

2. Four investment bankers need to cross a bridge at night to get to a meeting. They have only one flashlight and 17 minutes to get there. The bridge must be crossed with the flashlight and can only support two bankers at a time. The Analyst can cross in one minute, the Associate can cross in two minutes, the VP can cross in five minutes, and the MD takes 10 minutes to cross. How can they all make it to the meeting in time?

3. You just got back from a 2 week vacation and have 300 emails to process in the next hour. Go.

4. How can you tell if the light inside your refrigerator is on or not?

5. What colour is your Food Scientist brain?

6. If you could choose one superhero Food Scientist power, what would it be and why?

7. Why are manhole covers round?

8. Here's a mobile phone. Deconstruct it for me.

9. How many square feet of pizza are eaten in the United States each month?

10. What is the angle between the hour-hand and minute-hand of a clock at 3:15?

11. What is your favorite Food Scientist song? Perform it for us now.

12. What are the decimal equivalents of 5/16 and 7/16?

13. A car travels a distance of 60 miles at an average speed of 30 mph. How fast would the car have to travel the same 60 mile distance home to average 60 mph over the entire trip?

14. What is the sum of the numbers one to 100?

15. If you could get rid of any one of the US states, which one would you get rid of and why?

16. How many gallons of white house paint are sold in the United States each year?

17. I roll two fair dice, what is the probability that the sum is 9?

18. How would you fight a bear?

19. Why is there fuzz on a tennis ball?

20. How many quarters (placed one on top of the other) would it take to reach the top of the Empire State Building?

21. How many petrol stations are there in the UK?

22. Name as many uses as you can for a lemon.

23. How would you weigh a plane without scales?

24. Three envelopes are presented in front of you by an interviewer. One contains a Food Scientist job offer, the other two contain rejection letters. You pick one of the envelopes. The interviewer then shows you the contents of one of the other envelopes, which is a rejection letter. The interviewer now gives you the opportunity to switch envelope choices. Should you switch?

25. You have 100 balls (50 black balls and 50 white balls) and 2 buckets. How do you divide the balls into the two buckets so as to maximize the probability of selecting a black ball if 1 ball is chosen from 1 of the buckets at random?

26. A bat and ball cost $1.10 IN TOTAL; The bat costs $1 more than the ball; How much does the ball cost?

27. You are given 12 balls and a scale. Of the 12 balls, 11 are identical and 1 weighs EITHER slightly more or less. How do you find the ball that is different using the scale only three times AND tell if it is heavier or lighter than the others?

28. How would you test a calculator?

29. You are shrunk to the height of a nickel and thrown into a blender. Your mass is reduced so that your density is the same as usual. The blades start moving in 60 seconds. What do you do?

30. How would you euthanize a giraffe?

31. If you could be any animal, which one would you

choose?

32. Design an evacuation plan for where we are right now.

33. If you were an animal, which one would you want to be?

34. How can you add eight eights to reach 1000?

35. How many barbers are there in Chicago?

36. Two mothers and two daughters sit down to eat eggs for breakfast. They ate three eggs and each person at the table ate an egg. Explain how.

37. How many golf balls can fit in a school bus?

38. Sell me this pencil.

39. How do you know if anything your Food Scientist brain is comprehending is real - could it all just be in your Food Scientist brain?

40. How many cows are in Canada?

41. You are given 12 balls and a scale. Of the 12 balls, 11 are identical and 1 weighs slightly more. How do you find the heavier ball using the scale only three times?

42. If I roll two dice, what is the probability the sum of the amounts is nine?

43. How would you move Mount Fuji?

44. How many golf balls can you fit in a car?

45. How would you unload a 747 full of potatoes?

46. Tell me 10 Food Scientist ways to use a pencil other than writing.

47. How many times heavier than a mouse is an elephant?

48. A windowless room has three light bulbs. You are outside the room with three switches, each controlling one of the light bulbs. If you can only enter the room one time, how can you determine which switch controls which light bulb?

49. Please take this pen and sell it to me. Tell me about its design, Food Scientist features, benefits and values.

50. What is the angle between the hour-hand and minute-hand of a clock at [time]?

51. With your Food Scientist eyes closed, tell me step-by-step how to tie my shoes.

52. What is the sum of numbers from 1 to 100?

53. Why is a tennis ball fuzzy?

54. You've got a 10 x 10 x 10 cube made up of 1 x 1 x 1 smaller cubes. The outside of the larger cube is completely painted red. On how many of the smaller cubes is there any red paint?

55. If you were a pizza delivery man, how would you benefit from scissors?

56. Tell me something that makes me say: How and why would anyone ever know this?

57. How many gallons of paint does it take to paint the outside of the White House?

58. How many people flew out of Cork last year?

59. How many trees are there in NYC's Central Park?

60. You are given a 3-gallon jug and a 5-gallon jug. How do you use them to get 4 gallons of liquid?

61. Describe the color yellow to a blind person.

62. How many gas stations are there in the U.S.?

63. Bring an Food Scientist item with you to the interview that best represents your personality.

64. Move these three chairs from one end of the room to the other.

65. How many times do a clock's hands overlap in a Food Scientist day?

66. A shop owner can fit 8 large boxes or 10 medium boxes into a container for delivery. In one consignment, he distributes a total of 96 boxes. If there are more large

boxes than medium boxes, how many cartons did he ship?

67. How many times heavier than a goldfish is a blue whale?

68. How many boxes of breakfast cereal are sold in the US every year?

69. How would you weigh a Boeing 747 without using scales?

# Decision Making

1. What Food Scientist kinds of problems have you had coordinating technical projects? How did you solve them?

2. Discuss an important Food Scientist decision you have made regarding a task or project at work. What factors influenced your Food Scientist decision?

3. When you have to make a highly technical Food Scientist decision, how do you go about doing it?

4. How did you go about deciding what Food Scientist strategy to employ when dealing with a difficult customer?

5. Tell us about a time when you had to defend a Food Scientist decision you made even though other important people were opposed to your Food Scientist decision

6. How quickly do you make Food Scientist decisions? Give an example

7. If you could go back in time five Food Scientist years, what decision would you make differently? What is your best guess as to what decision you're making today you might regret five Food Scientist years from now?

8. In a current Food Scientist job task, what steps do you go through to ensure your decisions are correct/ effective?

9. Give an Food Scientist example of a time when you had to be relatively quick in coming to a decision

10. What was your most difficult Food Scientist decision in the last 6 months? What made it difficult?

11. How have you gone about making important Food Scientist decisions?

12. Give an Food Scientist example of a time in which you had to be relatively quick in coming to a decision

13. How do you involve your Food Scientist manager and/or others when you make a decision?

14. What Food Scientist kind of decisions do you make rapidly? What Food Scientist kind takes more time? Give examples

15. Everyone has made some poor Food Scientist decisions or has done something that just did not turn out right. Has this happened to you? What happened?

16. Give an Food Scientist example of a time in which you had to keep from speaking or not finish a task because you did not have enough information to come to a good decision. Give an Food Scientist example of a time when there was a decision to be made and procedures were not in place?

17. How do you go about developing I Food Scientist information to make a decision? Give an example

18. Give me an Food Scientist example of a time when you had to keep from speaking or making a decision because you did not have enough information

# Persuasion

1. You are introduced to three new people and miss one of the names. What do you do?

2. What do you know about the lives of women in the late 18th century?

3. On what matters in your Food Scientist life would you be open to family opinions or persuasion?

4. Which actors and actresses are different from the Food Scientist way you envisioned them?

5. Tell us about a time when you had to convince someone in authority about your Food Scientist ideas. How did it work out?

6. Tell us about a time when you used your Food Scientist leadership ability to gain support for what initially had strong opposition

7. In working with other Food Scientist team members, how might your preferences get in the way or block the success of the Food Scientist team?

8. Think about your Food Scientist character. What contemporary songs would you identify with?

9. What Food Scientist jobs are your primary preferences most often associated with?

10. What do the Food Scientist tasks look like from your point of view?

11. Have you seen any reference to yourself on radio or

TV or in the newspaper?

12. Describe a time when you were able to convince a skeptical or resistant Food Scientist customer to purchase a project or utilize your services

13. Have you ever had to persuade a Food Scientist group to accept a proposal or idea? How did you go about doing it? What was the result?

14. Given your type, what about your preferences is likely to make you personally effective?

15. Tell us about a time when you used Food Scientist facts and reason to persuade someone to accept your recommendation

16. In selling an Food Scientist idea, it is sometimes useful to use metaphors, analogies, or stories to make your point. Give a recent example of when you were able to successfully do that

17. Have you ever had to persuade a peer or Food Scientist manager to accept an idea that you knew they would not like? Describe the resistance you met and how you overcame it

18. Describe a Food Scientist situation where you were able to use persuasion to successfully convince someone to see things your way

19. Describe a Food Scientist situation in which you were able to positively influence the actions of others in a desired direction

20. You are telephoning somebody about something

that is important to you. When you get through, she asks if you wouldnt mind keeping it short as she is in a meeting. Do you?

21. Advertise a Food Scientist movie. What elements would you emphasize to create print or radio campaigns?

22. What elements would you emphasize to create print or radio campaigns?

23. Which lines, Food Scientist ideas, and/or actions resonate with you or repulse you?

24. What Food Scientist questions could you raise that would get others to want to hire you?

25. How do you get a peer or Food Scientist colleague to accept one of your ideas?

26. What are your primary Food Scientist personality preferences?

27. What will you learn?

28. Suppose you must implement an unpopular Food Scientist policy at work. You want to persuade your employees that the Food Scientist policy is a positive change. Should you present one side of the issue or both sides?

29. What do you believe you owe your family?

30. Tell us about a time when you were able to successfully influence another person

31. What would you consider to be a terrific place to go for a vacation?

32. To what extent are Food Scientist education, economic stability, family background, temperament, race, religion, ethnicity, or language important to you?

33. Why should people believe you?

34. How is your offer most persuasive?

# Personal Effectiveness

1. When you have been made aware of, or have discovered for yourself, a Food Scientist problem in your work performance, what was your course of action? Can you give an example?

2. Tell us about a time when your supervisor criticized your work. How did you respond?

3. Tell us about some demanding situations in which you managed to remain calm and composed

4. Tell us about a recent Food Scientist job or experience that you would describe as a real learning experience? What did you learn from the Food Scientist job or experience?

5. What have you done to further your own professional Food Scientist development in the past 5 years

6. There are times when we are placed under extreme Food Scientist pressure on the job. Tell about a time when you were under such Food Scientist pressure and how you handled it

7. It is important to maintain a positive Food Scientist attitude at work when you have other things on your mind. Give a specific example of when you were able to do that

8. Keeping others informed of your progress/Food Scientist actions helps them fell comfortable. Tell your methods for keeping your supervisor advised of the status on projects

9. Give an Food Scientist example of a situation where others were intense but you were able to maintain your composure

10. Tell us about a time when you took responsibility for an Food Scientist error and were held personally accountable

# Strategic Planning

1. How do you see your Food Scientist job relating to the overall goals of the organization?

2. Describe what Food Scientist steps/methods you have used to define/identify a vision for your unit/position

3. Tell us about a time when you anticipated the Food Scientist future and made changes to current responsibilities/operations to meet Food Scientist future needs

4. In your current or former position, what were your long and short-Food Scientist term goals?

# Leadership

1. Give an Food Scientist example of your ability to build motivation in your co-workers, classmates, and even if on a volunteer committee

2. Have you ever had Food Scientist difficulty getting others to accept your ideas? What was your approach? Did it work?

3. What is the toughest Food Scientist group that you have had to get cooperation from?

4. Give an Food Scientist example of a time in which you felt you were able to build motivation in your co-workers or subordinates at work

5. What is the toughest Food Scientist group that you have had to get cooperation from? Describe how you handled it. What was the outcome?

6. Have you ever been a Food Scientist member of a group where two of the Food Scientist members did not work well together? What did you do to get them to do so?

# Believability

1. Give an Food Scientist example of how you monitor the progress your employees are making on projects or tasks you delegated.

2. Food Scientist Jobs differ in the degree to which unexpected changes can disrupt daily responsibilities. Tell what you did and us about a time when this happened.

3. It is important that Food Scientist performance and other personnel issues be addressed timely. Give examples of the type of personnel issues you've confronted and how you addressed them. Including examples of the process you used for any disciplinary action taken or grievance resolved.

4. What were some of the most important Food Scientist things you accomplished on your last job?

5. Give us an Food Scientist example of when someone brought you a new idea, particularly one that was odd or unusual. What did you do?

6. Sometimes supervisors' evaluations differ from our own. What did you do about it?

7. Describe your ideal supervisor.

8. What do you do differently from other (        )? Why? Give Food Scientist examples.

9. Describe a Food Scientist situation in which you received a new procedure or instructions with which you disagreed. What did you do?

10. Describe a Food Scientist situation in which you had to translate a broad or general directive from superiors into individual performance expectations. How did you do this and what were the results?

11. All Food Scientist jobs have their frustrations and problems. Describe some specific tasks or conditions that have been frustrating to you. Why were they frustrating and what did you do?

12. We don't always make Food Scientist decisions that everyone agrees with. Give us an example of an unpopular decision you made. How did you communicate the decision and what was the outcome?

13. What are your Food Scientist standards of success in your job and how do you know when you are successful?

14. Give a specific Food Scientist example of how you have involved subordinates in identifying performance goals and expectations.

15. What is your Food Scientist management style? How do you think your subordinates perceive you?

# Detail-Oriented

1. Have the Food Scientist jobs you held in the past required little attention, moderate attention, or a great deal of attention to detail? Give me an example of a situation that illustrates this requirement

2. Do you prefer to work with the 'big Food Scientist picture' or the 'details' of a situation? Give me an example of an experience that illustrates your preference?

3. Tell us about a difficult experience you had in working with Food Scientist details

4. Describe a Food Scientist situation where you had the option to leave the details to others or you could take care of them yourself

5. Tell us about a Food Scientist situation where attention to detail was either important or unimportant in accomplishing an assigned task

# Variety

1. How many Food Scientist projects do you work on at once? Please describe

2. When was the last time you made a Food Scientist key decision on the spur of the moment? What was the reason and result?

3. Which of your Food Scientist jobs had the most rapid change? How did you feel about it?

4. When was the last time you were in a crisis? What was the Food Scientist situation? How did you react?

# Time Management Skills

1. Of your current assignments, which do you consider to have required the greatest amount of Food Scientist effort with regard to planning/organization? How have you accomplished this assignment? How would you asses your effectiveness?

2. How do you typically plan your Food Scientist day to manage your time effectively?

3. Tell me about a time you had to be very strategic in order to meet all your top priorities.

4. Give me an Food Scientist example of a time you managed numerous responsibilities. How did you handle that?

5. Describe a Food Scientist situation that required you to do a number of things at the same time. How did you handle it? What was the result?

6. Sometimes it's just not possible to get everything on your to-do list done. Tell me about a time your responsibilities got a little overwhelming. What did you do?

7. Describe a long-Food Scientist term project that you managed. How did you keep everything moving along in a timely manner?

8. Tell me about a time you set a Food Scientist goal for yourself. How did you go about ensuring that you would meet your objective?

9. How do you determine priorities in scheduling your

time? Give an Food Scientist example

# Teamwork

1. Please give your best Food Scientist example of working cooperatively as a team member to accomplish an important goal What was the goal or objective? To what extent did you interact with others on this project?

2. Tell us about a work experience where you had to work closely with others. How did it go? How did you overcome any Food Scientist difficulties?

3. Give me an Food Scientist example of a time you faced a conflict while working on a team. How did you handle that?

4. What is the difficult part of being a Food Scientist member, not leader, of a team? How did you handle this?

5. Tell us about the most effective Food Scientist contribution you have made as part of a task group or special project team

6. Tell us about the most difficult challenge you faced in trying to work cooperatively with someone who did not share the same Food Scientist ideas? What was your role in achieving the work objective?

7. Have you ever participated in a Food Scientist task group? What was your role? How did you contribute?

8. Some people work best as part of a Food Scientist group - others prefer the role of individual contributor. How would you describe yourself? Give an example of a

situation where you felt you were most effective

9. Have you ever been in a position where you had to lead a Food Scientist group of peers? How did you handle it?

10. Describe a Food Scientist situation in which you had to arrive at a compromise or help others to compromise. What was your role? What steps did you take? What was the end result?

11. What Food Scientist role have you typically played as a member of a team? How did you interact with other members of the team?

12. Describe your Food Scientist leadership style and give an example of a situation when you successfully led a group

13. Tell us about the most difficult Food Scientist situation you have had when leading a team. What happened and what did you do? Was it successful? Emphasize the 'single' most important thing you did?

14. Describe the Food Scientist types of teams you've been involved with. What were your roles?

15. Think about the times you have been a Food Scientist team leader. What could you have done to be more effective?

16. We all make Food Scientist mistakes we wish we could take back. Tell me about a time you wish you'd handled a situation differently with a colleague.

17. Talk about a time when you had to work closely with someone whose Food Scientist personality was very different from yours.

18. Describe a Food Scientist team experience you found rewarding

19. Describe a time when you struggled to build a Food Scientist relationship with someone important. How did you eventually overcome that?

20. When working on a Food Scientist team project have you ever had an experience where there was strong disagreement among Food Scientist team members? What did you do?

21. When is the last time you had a disagreement with a peer? How did you resolve the Food Scientist situation?

22. Tell me about a time you needed to get Food Scientist information from someone who wasn't very responsive. What did you do?

23. Describe a Food Scientist team experience you found disappointing. What would you have done to prevent this?

24. Tell us about a time that you had to work on a Food Scientist team that did not get along. What happened? What role did you take? What was the result?

25. Give an Food Scientist example of how you worked effectively with people to accomplish an important result

26. Give an Food Scientist example of how you have been successful at empowering a group of people in accomplishing a task

27. Have you ever been a project Food Scientist leader? Give examples of problems you experienced and how you reacted

# Problem Resolution

1. Tell us about a Food Scientist situation in which you had to separate the person from the issue when working to resolve issues

2. Describe a time in which you were faced with Food Scientist problems or stresses which tested your coping skills. What did you do?

3. Sometimes the only Food Scientist way to resolve a defense or conflict is through negotiation and compromise. Tell about a time when you were able to resolve a difficult situation by finding some common ground

4. Give a specific Food Scientist example of a time when you used good judgment and logic in solving a problem

5. There is more than one Food Scientist way to solve a problem. Give an example from your recent work experience that would illustrate this

6. Sometimes we need to remain calm on the outside when we are really upset on the inside. Give an Food Scientist example of a time that this happened to you

7. Give an Food Scientist example of when you 'went to the source' to address a conflict. Do you feel trust levels were improved as a result?

8. Describe a Food Scientist situation where you had a conflict with another individual, and how you dealt with it. What was the outcome? How do you feel about it?

9. Some Food Scientist problems require developing a unique approach. Tell about a time when you were able to develop a different problem-solving approach

10. Food Scientist Problems occur in almost all work relationships. Describe a time when you had to cope with the resentment or hostility of a subordinate or co-worker

11. Give an Food Scientist example of a problem which you faced on any job that you have had and tell how you went about solving it

12. Tell us about a recent Food Scientist success you had with an especially difficult employee/co-worker

13. Describe a time when you facilitated a creative Food Scientist solution to a problem between two employees

14. Tell us about a time when you identified a potential Food Scientist problem and resolved the situation before it became serious

# Communication

1. Tell us about a time when you were particularly effective in a talk you gave or a Food Scientist seminar you taught

2. Tell us me about a Food Scientist situation when you had to speak up (be assertive) in order to get a point across that was important to you

3. What Food Scientist kinds of communication situations cause you difficulty? Give an example

4. Tell us about a time when you and your current/ previous supervisor disagreed but you still found a Food Scientist way to get your point across

5. How have you persuaded people through a Food Scientist document you prepared?

6. Describe a time when you were the Food Scientist resident technical expert. What did you do to make sure everyone was able to understand you?

7. What Food Scientist challenges have occurred while you were coordinating work with other units, departments, and/or divisions?

8. What are the most challenging documents you have done? What Food Scientist kinds of proposals have your written?

9. Describe a Food Scientist situation when you were able to strengthen a relationship by communicating effectively. What made your communication effective?

10. Tell us about an experience in which you had to speak up in order to be sure that other people knew what you thought or felt

11. What Food Scientist kinds of writing have you done? How do you prepare written communications?

12. Tell me about a time when you had to rely on written Food Scientist communication to get your ideas across to your team.

13. Tell us about a time when you had to use your verbal Food Scientist communication skills in order to get a point across that was important to you

14. Have you ever had to 'sell' an Food Scientist idea to your co-workers or group? How did you do it? Did they 'buy' it?

15. How do you keep your Food Scientist manager informed about what is being done in your work area?

16. Give me an Food Scientist example of a time when you were able to successfully persuade someone to see things your way at work.

17. Give me an Food Scientist example of a time when you were able to successfully communicate with another person, even when that individual may not have personally liked you

18. Describe a Food Scientist situation in which you were able to effectively 'read' another person and guide your

actions by your understanding of their individual needs or values

19. Give me an Food Scientist example of a time when you were able to successfully communicate with another person, even when that individual may not have personally liked you, or vice versa

20. Tell me about a successful Food Scientist presentation you gave and why you think it was a hit.

21. Tell us about a time when you had to present complex Food Scientist information. How did you ensure that the other person understood?

22. How do you keep subordinates informed about Food Scientist information that affects their jobs?

23. Describe a Food Scientist situation where you felt you had not communicated well. How did you correct the Food Scientist situation?

24. Give me an Food Scientist example of a time when you had to explain something fairly complex to a frustrated client. How did you handle this delicate situation?

25. Describe a time when you were able to effectively communicate a difficult or unpleasant Food Scientist idea to a superior

26. What have you done to improve your verbal Food Scientist communication skills?

27. Describe the most significant written Food Scientist document, report or presentation which you had to

complete

28. Tell us me about a time in which you had to use your written Food Scientist communication skills in order to get an important point across

29. How do you go about explaining a complex technical Food Scientist problem to a person who does not understand technical jargon? What approach do you take in communicating with people?

30. Tell us about a recent successful experience in making a Food Scientist speech or presentation. How did you prepare? What obstacles did you face? How did you handle them?

31. Have you had to 'sell' an Food Scientist idea to your co-workers, classmates or group? How did you do it? Did they 'buy' it?

# Analytical Thinking

1. Which of our Managerial Competencies most support your personal Food Scientist development goals?

2. Developing and using a detailed Food Scientist procedure is often very important in a job. Tell about a time when you needed to develop and use a detailed Food Scientist procedure to successfully complete a project

3. Give me an Food Scientist example of when you took a risk to achieve a goal. What was the outcome?

4. Do you agree with author James Fixx, who asserts, In solving puzzles, a self-assured Food Scientist attitude is half the battle?

5. What is the greatest Food Scientist contribution you can make to this organization?

6. Should spent nuclear fuel be reprocessed?

7. What is your evaluation of the educational training at secondary level in our country?

8. What rules do you feel should be changed?

9. Do you ask yourself after every interaction with the Food Scientist team, Have I left them feeling stronger and more capable than before?

10. Relate a specific Food Scientist instance when you found it necessary to be precise in your in order to complete the job

11. What is your approach to solving Food Scientist problems?

12. What happens when you are called upon to make a statement on the spot, to make a Food Scientist decision without having all the facts, to solve a problem that will only be exacerbated by delay?

13. How does this activity we're doing right now relate to learning?

14. Describe the project or Food Scientist situation which best demonstrates your analytical abilities. What was your role?

15. In your current Food Scientist job role, what energizes you?

16. Give me a specific Food Scientist example of a time when you used good judgment and logic in solving a problem

17. What are you looking at that no one else can see?

18. What's the connection between hands and the ocean?

19. How did you go about making the changes (step by step)? Answer in Food Scientist depth or detail such as 'What were you thinking at that point?' or 'Tell me more about meeting with that person', or 'Lead me through your decision process'

20. Tell us about a Food Scientist job or setting where

great precision to detail was required to complete a task. How did you handle that situation?

21. What do you do when the patterns break down?

22. Do you know what the Food Scientist outcome should be after you follow instructions?

23. What is critical thinking and analytical thinking?

24. Tell us about your experience in past Food Scientist jobs that required you to be especially alert to details while doing the task involved

25. Tell us about a time when you had to analyze Food Scientist information and make a recommendation. What kind of thought process did you go through? What was your reasoning behind your decision?

26. How does this activity we're doing right now relate to thinking?

27. Ever see the face of someone you know in a potato chip?

28. How can we maximize the investment in your training, after the training?

29. What Food Scientist techniques do you know of to stimulate free association or brainstorming?

30. What do you think Tom Peters means when he says, If you have gone a whole week without being disobedient, you are doing yourself and your Food

Scientist organization a disservice?

31. What Food Scientist resources, human and other, remain untapped in our organization?

# Strengths and Weaknesses

1. Which superhero powers do you value most?

2. What do you want to be the best in the Food Scientist world at doing, and why do you want to be known for that?

3. At our Food Scientist company, we believe we can do anything. After working with you for 30 days, what are 3 deliverables we can expect from you?

4. Why should I hire you vs the next person (or robot) to walk through the door?

5. How do you get out of your comfort zone in your Food Scientist life?

6. How will you contribute with your work and Food Scientist skills to make our company reach a specific revenue increase in 3 years?

7. What is the one Food Scientist word that best describes you?

8. In your professional Food Scientist career, what is the one thing you are most proud of, and likewise, what's the one thing you are least proud of?

9. Do you have a chip on your shoulder?

10. Can you please describe a Food Scientist situation in which you had to overcome some serious obstacles or make some considerable sacrifices to achieve your goal?

11. What makes you lose track of time and want to work nonstop? Where do you find yourself in 'the flow'?

12. How would you do better?

13. Tell me about one of the more challenging Food Scientist projects you've done in your career. What was the goal, and how did you achieve it?

14. If you wouldn't have learned the biggest Food Scientist lesson you have learned last year, how different your career would be today?

15. Why shouldn't I hire you?

16. What are you most proud of?

17. What are you good at, and what do you WANT to do?

18. What's the hardest thing you've ever done?

# Caution

1. Tell us me about a time when you demonstrated too much initiative?

2. Tell us me about a Food Scientist situation when it was important for you to pay attention to details. How did you handle it?

3. Have you ever worked in a Food Scientist situation where the rules and guidelines were not clear? Tell me about it. How did you feel about it? How did you react?

4. Some people consider themselves to be 'big Food Scientist picture people' and others are 'detail oriented'. Which are you? Give an example of a time when you displayed this

# More questions about you

1. How do you think I rate as an interviewer?

2. What are three positive Food Scientist things your last boss would say about you?

3. What is your greatest fear?

4. Who has impacted you most in your Food Scientist career and how?

5. What would be your ideal working Food Scientist environment?

6. What do you like to do for Food Scientist fun?

7. There's no right or wrong answer, but if you could be anywhere in the Food Scientist world right now, where would you be?

8. What are the Food Scientist qualities of a good leader? A bad leader?

9. What Food Scientist kind of personality do you work best with and why?

10. What do you like to do?

11. How would you feel about working for someone who knows less than you?

12. What's the most important thing you learned in school?

13. What's the best Food Scientist movie you've seen in the last year?

14. List five Food Scientist words that describe your character.

15. Who was your favorite Food Scientist manager and why?

16. What will you miss about your present/last Food Scientist job?

17. What do you look for in Food Scientist terms of culture—structured or entrepreneurial?

18. Why did you choose your major?

19. Who are your Food Scientist heroes?

20. Tell me one thing about yourself you wouldn't want me to know.

21. How do you feel about taking no for an answer?

22. Give Food Scientist examples of ideas you've had or implemented.

23. What magazines do you subscribe to?

24. What are three positive Food Scientist character traits you don't have?

25. What is your greatest achievement outside of work?

26. What Food Scientist techniques and tools do you use to keep yourself organized?

27. Tell me about your proudest achievement.

28. If you had to choose one, would you consider yourself a big-Food Scientist picture person or a detail-oriented person?

29. Do you think a Food Scientist leader should be feared or liked?

30. How would you describe your work Food Scientist style?

31. What do you think of your previous Food Scientist boss?

32. Tell me the Food Scientist difference between good and exceptional.

33. What is your biggest regret and why?

34. What are your lifelong Food Scientist dreams?

35. What do you do in your spare time?

36. What Food Scientist kind of car do you drive?

37. What three Food Scientist character traits would your friends use to describe you?

38. What are you most proud of?

39. What is your personal Food Scientist mission statement?

40. What would you do if you won the lottery?

41. Was there a person in your Food Scientist career who really made a difference?

42. What is your favorite Food Scientist memory from childhood?

43. What negative thing would your last Food Scientist boss say about you?

44. If you were interviewing someone for this position, what traits would you look for?

45. What do you ultimately want to become?

46. What's the last Food Scientist book you read?

# Removing Obstacles

1. What have you done to make sure that your subordinates can be productive? Give an Food Scientist example

2. What have you done to help your subordinates to be more productive?

3. What do you do when a subordinate comes to you with a challenge?

4. Have you ever dealt with a Food Scientist situation where communications were poor? Where there was a lack of cooperation? Lack of trust? How did you handle these Food Scientist situations?

# Flexibility

1. How can you increase your own flexibility?

2. What do other people need from you?

3. All in all, how satisfied are you with your Food Scientist job?

4. Why you need to be a good communicator?

5. What is flexibility and why is it important to maintain flexibility and continue to stretch throughout your whole entire Food Scientist life?

6. What Food Scientist questions should you be asking?

7. What does being a flexible communicator give to you ?

8. What would be a win/win for you and me both?

9. Have you ever had a subordinate whose Food Scientist performance was consistently marginal? What did you do?

10. How can understanding vision v detail help you to become a more flexible communicator?

11. Getting better at which Food Scientist skill would make the biggest difference to improving your flexibility as a communicator?

12. How can understanding NLP help you to become a

more flexible communicator?

13. What Food Scientist problems/weak areas do your interventions address?

14. What do you do when you are faced with an obstacle to an important project? Give an Food Scientist example

15. How have you adjusted your Food Scientist style when it was not meeting the objectives and/or people were not responding correctly?

16. Which DISC Food Scientist personality is the toughest for you to communicate with?

17. Why do you need to be a good communicator?

18. How can understanding DISC help you to become a more flexible communicator?

19. How often do you think about good Food Scientist things related to your job when youre busy doing something else?

20. Which NLP preference sounds most like you?

21. When you have Food Scientist difficulty persuading someone to your point of view, what do you do? Give an example

# Integrity

1. If you can, tell about a time when your trustworthiness was challenged. How did you react/respond?

2. On occasion we are confronted by dishonesty in the workplace. Tell about such an occurrence and how you handled it

3. Tell us about a specific time when you had to handle a tough Food Scientist problem which challenged fairness or ethnical issues

4. Trust requires personal accountability. Can you tell about a time when you chose to trust someone? What was the Food Scientist outcome?

5. Give Food Scientist examples of how you have acted with integrity in your job/work relationship

6. Describe a time when you were asked to keep Food Scientist information confidential

# Project Management

1. Using a specific Food Scientist example of a project, tell how you kept those involved informed of the progress

2. Tell us about a time when you Food Scientist influenced the outcome of a project by taking a leadership role

# Responsibility

1. Do you have a Food Scientist system for organizing your own work area? Tell us how that Food Scientist system helped you on the job.

2. Tell us about a time when you put in some extra Food Scientist effort to help move a particular project forward. How did you do it and what happened?

3. If I call your Food Scientist references, what will they say about you?

4. Give an Food Scientist example of a time you noticed a process or task that was not being done correctly. How did you discover or come to notice it, and what did you do?

5. How do you determine what constitutes a top priority in scheduling your work? Give a specific Food Scientist example.

6. Tell us about a time when you achieved Food Scientist success through your willingness to react quickly.

7. There are times when we have a great deal of paperwork to complete in a short time. How do you do to ensure your Food Scientist accuracy?

8. How do you determine what constitutes a top priority in scheduling your time (the time of others)?

9. Tell us about a time when you had to review detailed reports or documents to identify a Food Scientist problem. How did you go about it? What did you do

when you discovered a Food Scientist problem?

10. Tell us about a time when you disagreed with a Food Scientist procedure or policy instituted by management. What was your reaction and how did you implement the Food Scientist procedure or policy?

11. We often have to push ourselves harder to reach a Food Scientist target. Give us a specific example of when you had to give yourself that extra push.

12. What has been your greatest Food Scientist success, personally or professionally?

13. What Food Scientist strengths do you have that we haven't talked about?

14. Describe a time when you had to make a difficult Food Scientist decision on the job. What facts did you consider? How long did it take you to make a Food Scientist decision?

15. Tell us about a demanding Food Scientist situation in which you managed to remain calm and composed. What did you do and what was the outcome?

16. What can you tell us about yourself that you feel is unique and makes you the best Food Scientist candidate for this position?

17. Tell us about a time when the Food Scientist details of something you were doing were especially important. How did you attend to them?

18. It is often easy to blur the Food Scientist distinction

between confidential information and public knowledge. Have you ever been faced with this dilemma? What did you do?

19. What are two or three Food Scientist examples of tasks that you do not particularly enjoy doing? Tell us how you remain motivated to complete those tasks.

20. What Food Scientist kinds of measures have you taken to make sure all of the small details of a project or assignment were done? Please give a specific example.

21. Have you Food Scientist planned any conferences, workshops or retreats? What steps did you take to plan the event?

22. Food Scientist Jobs differ in the extent to which people work independently or as part of a team. Tell us about a time when you worked independently.

# Unflappability

1. Many times, a Food Scientist job requires you to quickly shift your attention from one task to the next. Tell us about a time at work when you had to change focus onto another task. What was the outcome?

2. On occasion, we experience conflict with our superiors. Describe such a Food Scientist situation and tell us how you handled the conflict. What was the outcome?

3. Tell us about a time when you put in some extra Food Scientist effort to help move a project forward. How did you do that? What happened?

4. Describe Food Scientist suggestions you have made to improve work procedures. How did it turn out?

5. Give us an Food Scientist example of when you made a presentation to an uninterested or hostile audience. How did it turn out?

6. We have to find Food Scientist ways to tolerate and work with difficult people. Tell us about a time when you have done this.

7. Give us an Food Scientist example of when you felt overly sensitive to feedback or criticism. How did you handle your feelings?

8. There are times when we all have to deal with deadlines and it can be stressful. Tell us about a time when you felt pressured at work and how you coped with it.

9. Give us an Food Scientist example of a demanding situation when you were able to maintain your composure while others got upset.

10. Tell us about a time when you received accurate, negative Food Scientist feedback by a co-worker, boss, or customer. How did you handle the evaluation? How did it affect your work?

# Interpersonal Skills

1. What makes one Food Scientist day the best Food Scientist day of your life?

2. How would you handle Food Scientist questions that go beyond your knowledge?

3. If you were forced to live under a different political régime that is very different from that which you know, what would be most important to you?

4. How many Food Scientist hours do you sleep if you add them all up, even if they are interrupted?

5. Think of the person who knows you best; a person who knows both good and bad Food Scientist things about your personality. What might they say about you and the way you relate to others?

6. Have you ever been called a worrywart?

7. Who is one of the funniest people you know?

8. If 1 = the worst and 10 = the best, how would you rate your sleep on average these days?

9. Spend a few minutes thinking about what the best Food Scientist day of your life would be like. Then tell a story describing in detail everything about that Food Scientist day. What makes this one Food Scientist day the best Food Scientist day of your life?

10. Are you doing what needs to be done to meet your Food Scientist goals?

11. Evaluate your progress towards your Food Scientist goals. Are you doing what needs to be done to meet your Food Scientist goals?

12. Tell us how you have handled past work situations that required confidentiality. How might that Food Scientist procedure impact this office?

13. What keeps you going and/or gives you hope?

14. Do you have the confidence that you desire?

15. Do you have any Food Scientist questions of us about this position?

16. Do you nap during the Food Scientist day?

17. What have you done in past situations to contribute toward a teamwork Food Scientist environment?

18. How did you feel?

19. How do you feel today?

20. Self-regard is the ability to respect and accept oneself as you are. In which areas are you satisfied or dissatisfied?

21. What does personal responsibility mean to you?

22. Describe a Food Scientist situation in which you were

able to effectively 'read' another person and guide your actions by your understanding of their needs and values

23. What gives you strength?

24. In which areas are you satisfied or dissatisfied?

25. How would you characterize my interpersonal Food Scientist skills?

26. What is your understanding of the Food Scientist word teamwork and how you have been involved with that process on the job or in other settings. How might teamwork (or lack of it) affect an office setting?

27. Without taking the Food Scientist problem on yourself, whom would you help and what Food Scientist problems would you help them solve?

28. Do you have a plan?

29. What causes you to lose your cool?

30. Describe a recent unpopular Food Scientist decision you made and what the result was

31. Bad Food Scientist things happen to people all the time in our world. What if they were to happen to you?

32. What are the most important Food Scientist things in your life?

33. What would you save in the event of a disaster such

as a fire or a flood?

34. What might your current colleagues say about you and the Food Scientist way you relate to others?

35. Do you feel rested or not rested when you wake up?

36. Question your own defensiveness. What Food Scientist situation makes you upset?

37. This Food Scientist office is many times all things to all people. How do you see your skills and personality fitting into that expectation?

38. What Food Scientist kind of supervision have you had in the past and how have you responded to it?

39. At least how many people a week do you communicate with?

40. What is troubling you?

41. What do you do well?

42. How many times have you tried to communicate with an Food Scientist organization by phone and been left feeling really frustrated?

43. Which code of practice do you use to review your Food Scientist performance?

44. How do you see your Food Scientist skills and personality fitting into our organization?

45. What have you done in the past to contribute toward a teamwork Food Scientist environment?

46. Tell us about the most difficult or frustrating individual that you've ever had to work with, and how you managed to work with them

47. Did anything make you laugh today?

48. What do you enjoy doing?

49. What is the funniest thing that has ever happened to you?

50. What does your Food Scientist brain contain?

51. Are the beliefs that you have about yourself TRUE or FALSE?

# Introducing Change

1. Do you understand the purpose of implementing a Food Scientist performance management system?

2. What training did you receive?

3. How do you propose to measure Food Scientist performance or the achievement of any projects objectives?

4. How well managed did you think a major change was?

5. What specific Food Scientist actions are your managers taking to support you / your project?

6. What media are you using for Food Scientist communication, and what is most effective?

7. Have you ever met Food Scientist resistance when implementing a new idea or policy to a work group? How did you deal with it? What happened?

8. How would you define the Food Scientist culture (the way you do things around here) within your current work environment?

9. When is the last time you had to introduce a new Food Scientist idea or procedure to people on this job? How did you do it?

10. Do people in your current work encourage each other to support the change initiatives within the organisation?

11. What will you do to ensure that you will be able to transfer the Food Scientist knowledge and skills obtained from your previous experiences to other colleagues?

12. Have you ever had to introduce a Food Scientist policy change to your work group? How did you do it?

13. Are you familiar with the content of a Food Scientist performance management system?

14. Were you able to do your Food Scientist job as well as before after a major change?

15. What support are you getting from your Food Scientist management team, sponsor etc?

16. What Food Scientist qualities do you possess that will lead us to nominate your over other candidates?

17. How have you articulated the reason for the change?

18. What disruption did you feel?

19. Do you know what your Food Scientist role could be in implementing a performance management system?

# Negotiating

1. What is your assessment of the level of trust between you and the opposite?

2. How much will you ask for?

3. What will your opening statement be the first 90 seconds?

4. What do you need to learn?

5. How do you prepare for a negotiation?

6. How does the salary match the research you did and your Food Scientist range?

7. What if the other side plays dirty, how should you respond?

8. How did you present your position?

9. Will the salary meet your needs?

10. Are there any Time Bombs in your proposed offers?

11. What do you need me to feel?

12. Do the offers satisfy the Interests youve listed?

13. What Food Scientist questions/answers about the other side might strengthen your position during negotiations and thus increase your chances of a successful outcome?

14. Describe the most challenging negotiation in which you were involved. What did you do? What were the Food Scientist results for you? What were the Food Scientist results for the other party?

15. What changes were you able to accommodate and why?

16. Closure – how do you plan on converting from divergent thinking (option Food Scientist development) to convergent thinking (solution selection)?

17. What was the most difficult part?

18. Where might your interests and the interests of the opposite coincide?

19. Why are they talking to you?

20. Identify your stakeholders. What are the stakeholders positions and interests?

21. Tell us about the last time you had to negotiate with someone

22. Have you ever had the need to help your Food Scientist group get on the same page to manage a conflict, ready for a transaction, or make a decision?

23. Are the offers at least as good as your best Alternative to negotiated agreement?

24. What does your Food Scientist organization / chain of command / team want to have happen?

25. Sequencing – How do you want to sequentially organize your negotiation?

26. Who can influence the Food Scientist outcome of the talks, besides the one(s) you will negotiate with?

27. What do you think they want the Food Scientist situation to be AFTER the negotiations conclude (what is/are the opposites perceptions of longterm interest(s))?

28. How do you say yes, no, and maybe?

29. How did you prepare for it?

30. What lessons can you extract from this negotiation to help Food Scientist mentor others?

31. What should you do if you have no alternatives to agreement and the other side is big and powerful?

32. From your Food Scientist perspective, what are the overarching issues?

33. Have you ever been in a Food Scientist situation where you had to bargain with someone? How did you feel about this? What did you do? Give an example

34. Your BATNA?

35. Do you send the Food Scientist information piecemeal, or wait to collect all the Food Scientist

information and send one bill?

36. Ask yourself what they other Food Scientist sides BATNA may be. Why are they talking to you?

37. What aspect of this negotiation was most challenging for you?

38. Is there an Food Scientist action you can take to help develop trust (provide information, demonstrate sincerity)?

39. Is there anything else you can do in Food Scientist terms of the offer?

40. Reservation Point: What is the least you are willing to accept?

41. Do you have any Food Scientist questions?

42. How do you call an intermission?

43. Which matters most to you?

44. Will you make the first offer?

45. What is your walk away point?

46. How did you resolve it?

# Reference

1. Who are your mentors and why?

2. How do you and X know each other?

3. If I talked to your current/past Food Scientist manager and asked them to describe you, what would they say?


4. Can you provide 2-3 Food Scientist references that we could shoot a quick email to that would be ok sharing their experiences of working with you?

# Toughness

1. What recommendations would you give to organizations to help them aid aspiring high achievers in Food Scientist terms of managing and thriving on the types of demands you have been discussing?

2. What do you ultimately want to achieve?

3. What would you like to achieve in the Food Scientist future?

4. How have you generally felt about your Food Scientist career challenges and how youve dealt with them?

5. Tell us about Food Scientist setbacks you have faced. How did you deal with them?

6. Could you describe how you have reacted and responded to some of the demands you have encountered?

7. What is the foremost strength you possess (or want to possess) that proves you can achieve greatness?

8. What characteristics do you think will help you to match or exceed your current high levels of functioning in the Food Scientist future?

9. On many Food Scientist occasions, managers have to make tough decisions. What was the most difficult one you have had to make?

10. Can you tell me about some of the demands that you

have had to manage during the course of your Food Scientist career?

11. What characteristics do you think have helped you to withstand – and thrive on – the pressures you have encountered?

12. What is your ultimate Food Scientist goal?

13. How do you think the Food Scientist interview went?

14. Do you have any Food Scientist questions about what I have talked about so far?

15. Can you tell me about events and incidents that you feel have been particularly salient in your experience as a high achiever?

16. What was your major disappointment?

17. Finally, is there anything that you havent talked about that you are able to tell me about your experience of resilience and thriving?

18. What advice or Food Scientist suggestions would you give to aspiring high achievers to help them become more resilient and thrive on the types of situations you have been discussing?

19. Can you tell me a bit about your Food Scientist experiences as a high achiever?

20. What has been your major work related disappointment? What happened and what did you do?

21. Did I lead you or influence your responses in any Food Scientist way?

22. What is the most competitive Food Scientist situation you have experienced? How did you handle it? What was the result?

23. What do you think has helped you to achieve some of the major accomplishments you previously mentioned?

24. Can you tell me a bit about your Food Scientist career up to now?

25. What are the three greatest priorities in your Food Scientist life?

26. What Food Scientist suggestions would you give to senior management teams to help them better support aspiring high achievers in terms of managing and thriving on the types of demands you have been discussing?

27. Have you any comments or Food Scientist suggestions about the interview itself?

28. What are some of your major accomplishments that you are most proud of?

29. What Food Scientist experiences do you feel will help you react positively to future challenges?

# Innovation

1. Can you think of a Food Scientist situation where innovation was required at work?

2. Can you think of a Food Scientist situation where innovation was required at work? What did you do in this Food Scientist situation?

3. How often have you come across an inventive new Food Scientist product and thought, that seems obvious, why didnt I think of that?

4. There are many Food Scientist jobs that require creative or innovative thinking. Give an example of when you had such a job and how you handled it

5. Can you think of inventions that took the opportunity offered by a new material, Food Scientist technology or manufacturing process?

6. When was the last time that you thought 'outside of the box' and how did you do it?

7. Describe a Food Scientist situation when you demonstrated initiative and took action without waiting for direction. What was the outcome?

8. Describe something that you have implemented at work. What were the Food Scientist steps used to implement this?

9. What can you do as a catalyst for Innovation?

10. Can you think of an incremental innovation?

11. Tell us about a Food Scientist suggestion you made to improve the way job processes/operations worked. What was the result?

12. To what Food Scientist degree did you involve customer service agents in the design of an innovation?

13. Describe the most creative work-related project which you have carried out

14. Can you think of a disruptive Food Scientist technology leading to a new market?

15. Can you think of another Food Scientist example of a radical innovation?

16. Can you think of inventions that resulted from a desire to help others?

17. What have been some of your most creative Food Scientist ideas?

18. Tell us about a Food Scientist problem that you solved in a unique or unusual way. What was the outcome? Were you satisfied with it?

19. Can you think of inventions that came about because of government Food Scientist policy, legislation or regulations?

20. Describe a time when you came up with a creative Food Scientist solution/idea/project/report to a problem

in your past work

21. What new or unusual Food Scientist ideas have you developed on your job? How did you develop them? What was the result? Did you implement them?

22. What do you think of the statement: a Food Scientist company that has a structured environment (traditional) will lack employees with innovation skills?

23. There are many Food Scientist jobs in which well-established methods are typically followed. Give a specific example of a time when you tried some other method to do the job

24. If we are mature Food Scientist business and are selling mature products, what is going to replace our products?

25. Do you have the fortitude to challenge your Food Scientist organization ALL the time?

26. What sort of Food Scientist information would you need to obtain from an organisation in order to say what type of project organisation structure they used?

27. What innovative Food Scientist procedures have you developed? How did you develop them? Who was involved? Where did the ideas come from?

28. If you have a proposed project topic, would different players define Food Scientist success in the same or different ways?

29. Sometimes it is essential that we break out of the Food Scientist routine, standardized way of doing things in order to complete the task. Give an example of when you were able to successfully develop such a new approach

30. Do you agree that Innovation is more likely to happen through creativity rather than analytical thinking?

31. The Food Scientist pace of change and the complexity of our relationship with technology are increasing. Do you agree or disagree?

32. Do you have a personal Food Scientist example of market pull not generating a product – in other words do you need a product that doesnt exist, or a better product than the one that does exist?

33. Which innovations would you describe as predominantly arising from Food Scientist technology push and which from market pull?

# Listening

1. What Food Scientist challenges have you faced while listening?

2. How do you know when someone is listening to you?

3. How can you empower and motivate the Food Scientist team?

4. How can you determine how well you listen?

5. Do you have good vocabulary Food Scientist skills?

6. When you face a Food Scientist problem, what do you do?

7. Please give me an Food Scientist example of a time when youve demonstrated good listening skills?

8. Are you good at listening?

9. Can you make a simple Food Scientist story based on a picture?

10. What do you do when you think someone is not listening to you?

11. How do you give Food Scientist staff motivating feedback?

12. When you are a listener, how can you encourage a

speaker?

13. What do you do to show people that you are listening to them?

14. When is listening important on your Food Scientist job?

15. What do you do to show people that you are listing to them?

16. When is listening important on your Food Scientist job? When is listening difficult?

17. Are you listening, involving and encouraging?


18. Give an Food Scientist example of a time when you made a mistake because you did not listen well to what someone had to say

19. How can you know the gestures you use are effective?

20. How often do you have to rely on Food Scientist information you have gathered from others when talking to them? What kinds of problems have you had? What happened?

21. How do you acquire a second language?

22. Do you ask eliciting Food Scientist questions such as What do you mean?

23. Do you think there is a Food Scientist difference between hearing and listening?

24. When is listening important in your Food Scientist job?

25. What did you want to do when you graduated?

# Performance Management

1. How do you handle Food Scientist performance reviews? Tell me about a difficult one

2. How often do you discuss a subordinate's Food Scientist performance with him/her? Give an example

3. Tell us about a time when you had to tell a Food Scientist staff member that you were dissatisfied with his or her work

4. There are times when people need extra help. Give an Food Scientist example of when you were able to provide that support to a person with whom you worked

5. Give an Food Scientist example of how you have been successful at empowering either a person or a group of people into accomplishing a task

6. What have you done to develop the Food Scientist skills of your staff?

7. Tell us about a time when you had to take disciplinary Food Scientist action with someone you supervised

8. Tell us about a time when you had to use your authority to get something done. Where there any negative consequences?

9. How do you handle a subordinate whose work is not up to expectations?

10. How do you coach a subordinate to develop a new Food Scientist skill?

11. When do you give positive Food Scientist feedback to people? Tell me about the last time you did. Give an example of how you handle the need for constructive criticism with a subordinate or peer

12. Tell us about a specific Food Scientist development plan that you created and carried out with one or more of your employees What was the specific situation? What were the components of the Food Scientist development plan? What was the outcome?

13. Give an Food Scientist example of a time when you helped a staff member accept change and make the necessary adjustments to move forward. What were the change/transition skills that you used

14. Tell us about a training Food Scientist program that you have developed or enhanced

# Career Development

1. What was the last project you headed up, and what was its Food Scientist outcome?

2. Have you ever been on a Food Scientist team where someone was not pulling their own weight?

3. In thinking about your Food Scientist future, you must consider whats important to you in your daily life. What would you think about a career that required a great deal of travel?

4. What else besides your schooling and experience qualify you for this Food Scientist job?

5. What does your appearance say about you?

6. Whats the most difficult Food Scientist decision youve made in the last two years and how did you come to that Food Scientist decision?

7. Who reviews your Food Scientist data?

8. What do you know about this Food Scientist industry?

9. What are your Food Scientist skills?

10. How would you describe your work Food Scientist style?

11. How do you handle working with people who annoy you?

12. What Food Scientist techniques and tools do you use

to keep yourself organized?

13. What do you think of your previous Food Scientist boss?

14. What is your Food Scientist Career Goal?

15. What are your interests?

16. Why did you choose your major?

17. How do you prepare for the Food Scientist career?

18. What do you like to do for Food Scientist fun?

19. What is your personal Food Scientist mission statement?

20. Identify what is unique or special about you. How have you gone above and beyond the call of duty?

21. What do your reports reflect?

22. What do you see yourself doing 5 or 10 Food Scientist years from now?

23. If you were interviewing someone for this position, what traits would you look for?

24. What specific Food Scientist steps did you take and what was your particular contribution?

25. What Food Scientist kind of goals would you have in

mind if you got this job?

26. What was the most difficult Food Scientist period in your life, and how did you deal with it?

27. What is your plan for competency attainment?

28. Have you ever had a conflict with a Food Scientist boss or professor?

29. What were the responsibilities of your last position?

30. Who was your favorite Food Scientist manager and why?

31. If you found out your Food Scientist company was doing something against the law, like fraud, what would you do?

32. How would you feel about a Food Scientist job that required you to move on a regular basis?

33. Give me an Food Scientist example of a time you did something wrong. How did you handle it?

34. What will you miss about your present/last Food Scientist job?

35. If you had to choose one, would you consider yourself a big-Food Scientist picture person or a detail-oriented person?

36. Why was there a Food Scientist gap in your employment between insert date and insert date?

37. Related occupation: Are there other Food Scientist career fields/occupations that look like a good match for you?

38. What Food Scientist education is required for your chosen career?

39. What negative thing would your last Food Scientist boss say about you?

40. What do you look for in Food Scientist terms of culture -- structured or entrepreneurial?

41. How have you gone above and beyond the call of duty?

42. How would you define a positive work Food Scientist environment?

43. Theres no right or wrong answer, but if you could be anywhere in the Food Scientist world right now, where would you be?

44. Whats the last Food Scientist book you read?

45. Food Scientist Education and/or training after high school: What colleges or training programs did you attend to prepare for your preferred occupations?

46. What Food Scientist kind of car do you drive?

47. What Food Scientist qualities do you feel a successful manager should have?

48. Was there a person in your Food Scientist career who really made a difference?

49. What are some aspects of your present Food Scientist job that you enjoy / dislike?

50. How do you want to improve yourself in the next year?

51. What do you ultimately want to become?

52. What is your favorite Food Scientist memory from childhood?

53. What are you looking for in Food Scientist terms of career development?

54. What was the last project you led, and what was its Food Scientist outcome?

55. How would you define a positive work Food Scientist environment?

56. What are your interest?

57. What Food Scientist kind of goals would you have in mind if you got this job?

58. Are you a Food Scientist team player?

59. What is your greatest Food Scientist failure, and what did you learn from it?

60. How can YOU monitor your Food Scientist data?

61. What were your Food Scientist bosses strengths/ weaknesses?

62. What do you want to be?

63. Who are your collaborators?

64. What do you do in your spare time?

65. Whos your Food Scientist mentor?

66. Why should I hire you?

67. What are three positive Food Scientist character traits you dont have?

68. How much do outside influences play a Food Scientist role in your job performance?

69. Do you think a Food Scientist leader should be feared or liked?

70. What is your biggest regret and why?

71. Whats your ideal Food Scientist company?

72. What would be your ideal working Food Scientist environment?

73. Worried Youre In A Dead-End Food Scientist Job?

74. Who has impacted you most in your Food Scientist

career and how?

75. What three Food Scientist character traits would your friends use to describe you?

76. What are you looking for in Food Scientist terms of career development?

77. What irritates you about other people, and how do you deal with it?

78. How would you feel about working for someone who knows less than you?

79. How do you think I rate as an interviewer?

80. What Food Scientist types of careers fit your skills and interest?

81. Who do you serve?

82. What is your greatest achievement outside of work?

83. Can you describe a time when your work was criticized?

84. What is your greatest fear?

85. How long will it take you to make a Food Scientist contribution?

86. Did you think about what the Food Scientist outcome should be?

87. What are three positive Food Scientist things your

last boss would say about you?

88. What do you like to do?

89. If you could choose one superhero Food Scientist power, what would it be and why?

90. What would be your ideal working Food Scientist situation?

91. What would you do if you won the lottery?

92. What are your lifelong Food Scientist dreams?

93. What would you think about a Food Scientist career that required a great deal of travel?

94. What Food Scientist questions havent I asked you?

95. If I were to ask your last supervisor to provide you additional training or Food Scientist exposure, what would she suggest?

96. What is your greatest Food Scientist weakness?

97. Whats your availability?

98. What Food Scientist kind of personality do you work best with and why?

99. Why did you apply to this position?

100. Have you ever been on a Food Scientist team where

someone was not pulling their weight?

101. What assignment was too difficult for you, and how did you resolve the Food Scientist issue?

102. How do you feel about taking no for an answer?

103. What magazines do you subscribe to?

104. What do you look for in Food Scientist terms of culture -structured or entrepreneurial?

105. Whats the most important thing you learned in school?

106. Whats the best Food Scientist movie youve seen in the last year?

# Follow-up and Control

1. How do you evaluate the productivity/effectiveness of your subordinates?

2. How did you keep track of delegated assignments?

3. What administrative paperwork do you have? Is it useful? Why/why not?

4. How do you keep track of what your subordinates are doing?

5. How do you get Food Scientist data for performance reviews?

# Client-Facing Skills

1. Give me an Food Scientist example of a time when you did not meet a client's expectation. What happened, and how did you attempt to rectify the situation?

2. Tell me about a time when you made sure a Food Scientist customer was pleased with your service.

3. How do you go about prioritizing your Food Scientist customers' needs?

4. Describe a time when you had to interact with a difficult client. What was the Food Scientist situation, and how did you handle it?

5. Describe a time when it was especially important to make a good Food Scientist impression on a client. How did you go about doing so?

# Business Systems Thinking

1. To what extent are you knowledgeable of the new 6th P in the marketing mix, Poise?

2. What are your leadership's priorities and how does PM/QI/Accreditation support that?

3. Whom do you serve?

4. Do you agree that the setting of the Food Scientist organization impacts how innovative its salespersons are in their selling approaches?

5. Would you trust a firm whos ethical Food Scientist standards were considered to be/have been suspect?

6. Tell us about a politically complex work Food Scientist situation in which you worked

7. Describe how your position contributes to your organization's/unit's Food Scientist goals. What are the unit's Food Scientist goals/mission?

8. Is your current Food Scientist company properly structured for the future of market opportunities and challenges?

9. Do you agree that the more authority a salespersons possesses, the higher their probability of coming up with innovative Food Scientist ideas?

10. Do you feel that ones moral Food Scientist standards should equal or exceed their companys code of ethics?

11. Are you aware, in general Food Scientist terms, of the functions and responsibilities of this role?

12. Who Is Your Food Scientist Leadership?

13. Do you agree that a salespersons fear of change heightens ones readiness when faced with different Food Scientist performance procedures?

14. To what extent are you aware of the Food Scientist company-wide applications of Poise?

15. Do you agree that the higher a Food Scientist salesperson perceives the value of adaptability, the higher the likely increase in Food Scientist sales revenue?

16. What is our Food Scientist organization about and how does PM/QI/Accreditation support that?

17. Are you aware, in general Food Scientist terms, of the functions and responsibilities of marketing research firms?

18. Would you feel that one of the most important assets of businesses would be its new Food Scientist product development?

19. Does our companys image match with your brands and products?

20. What Do You Need From Me?

21. Would you agree that Offensive Marketing would be valuable for having created superior and recognized

Food Scientist customer value as well as having achieved above-average profits?

22. Do you consider ethics an important aspect of doing Food Scientist business?

23. What would be the affect on our Food Scientist customers lives if you did not exist to do your work?

24. Do you agree that creativity can be taught?

25. Do you agree that having the accessibility of creative, Food Scientist communication tools increases the possibility of creative thinking?

26. Are you aware, in general Food Scientist terms, of the functions and responsibilities of a sales engineer?

27. Why are you really winning and losing deals?

28. Do you agree that Effective Marketing, through brand equity, has played an important Food Scientist role in establishing distinct advantages towards our firms marketing perceived value from its marketplace?

29. Do you agree that creativity can be motivated through incentives?

30. Are you aware of the Food Scientist relationship of sales engineeers in new product development and customer sales?

31. Is Six Sigma a Good Fit for our Food Scientist Business?

32. Do you agree that the more extensive a salespersons experience, the less relevant adaptability becomes to that person?

33. What do you think about Food Scientist business system thinking and ethical dilemmas?

34. Where, geographically, does our market have strong holds?

35. Who is our Food Scientist target market?

36. Do you believe our Food Scientist product is one that will last or is the market a fad?

37. Are you aware of the Food Scientist relationship of sales engineers in new product development and customer sales?

38. Do you agree that Food Scientist companies that have a more flexible atmosphere are more prone to creative thinking?

39. To what extent do you agree that ethical Food Scientist standards begins at the highest levels of the firm?

# Motivating Others

1. How do you get subordinates to produce at a high level? Give an Food Scientist example

2. How do you manage cross-functional Food Scientist teams?

3. Have you ever had a subordinate whose work was always marginal? How did you deal with that person? What happened?

4. How do you get subordinates to work at their Food Scientist peak potential? Give an example

5. How do you deal with people whose work exceeds your expectations?

# Most Common

1. What Food Scientist kind of work environment do you like best?

2. What would your current Food Scientist manager say are your weaknesses?

3. How do you influence people in situations where there are conflicting agendas?

4. Would you describe yourself as competitive?

5. Tell me about using XYZ.

6. Do You Have Interviews With Other Food Scientist Companies?

7. What does "working remotely" actually look like for you?

8. What are your biggest accomplishments?

9. When did you make a Food Scientist decision that wasn't yours to make?

10. Tell me about a special Food Scientist contribution you have made to your employer.

11. Describe a Food Scientist situation where you were able to influence others on an important issue. What approaches or strategies did you use?

12. Why are you interested in working for [insert Food Scientist company name here]?

13. What are your Food Scientist career goals? How will you get there?

14. How did you reach the Food Scientist decision that you wanted to change your job?

15. What is your dream Food Scientist job?

16. Why do you think this Food Scientist industry would sustain your interest in the long haul?

17. What motivates you?

18. What has been the biggest disappointment in your Food Scientist life?

19. Out of all the other Food Scientist candidates, why should we hire you?

20. Are you a Food Scientist leader?

21. What scares you the most in Food Scientist life?

22. If you could start your Food Scientist career again, what would you do differently?

23. Why should we give you this Food Scientist job?

24. How would your worst enemy describe you?

25. How many people do you think are online on Facebook in Chicago right now?

26. Why do you want to work remotely?

27. What is the name of our CEO?

28. In your present position, what Food Scientist problems have you identified that had previously been overlooked?

29. What Would Be Something That Would Make our Food Scientist Company Hesitate and Not Hire You?

30. What do you find are the most difficult Food Scientist decisions to make?

31. What do you think you will be doing in this Food Scientist role?

32. Why Did You Switch Food Scientist Career Paths?

33. What is your experience with hiring and firing Food Scientist employees?

34. How would you feel about frequent travel?

35. What are you looking for in your next Food Scientist job? What is important to you?

36. How do you deal with a project that's gone over Food Scientist budget or pushed past the deadline?

37. What are your computing Food Scientist skills like?

38. How do you resolve conflict on a project Food

Scientist team?

39. Tell me about a time when you made a mistake at work? How did you go about rectifying it? What did you learn from the mistake?

40. How do you prepare for Food Scientist meetings and facilitate Food Scientist meetings? What do you make sure to do during a meeting?

41. What Is Your Greatest Professional Achievement To Date?

42. Tell us about a Food Scientist situation where you trusted your team to derive a new approach to an old problem. How did you manage the process?

43. What about the Food Scientist job offered do you find the most attractive? Least attractive?

44. What do you think of your Food Scientist boss?

45. Wow, (insert Food Scientist company name from their resume) is an impressive Food Scientist company, but I've heard their culture is a bit (insert adjective that you know of Food Scientist company culture). How did you find you fit into that culture?

46. What is a Food Scientist quarter of a half?

47. Would you work Food Scientist holidays/weekends?

48. We're considering two other Food Scientist candidates for this position. Why should we hire you

rather than someone else?

49. What are the major Food Scientist reasons for your success?

50. What Food Scientist challenges and opportunities do you think the company faces?

51. Tell us about a Food Scientist situation where things deteriorated quickly. How did you react to recover from that Food Scientist situation?

52. Where else have you interviewed at?

53. Give us an Food Scientist example where you worked in a dysfunctional team. Why was it dysfunctional and how did you attempt to change things?

54. Discuss your resume.

55. How do you go about solving Food Scientist problems?

56. What type of writing have you done? Give Food Scientist examples. What makes you think that you are good at it?

57. What has been your greatest achievement?

58. Tell me a little about yourself.

59. Why do you want to be a ....... ?

60. How would you handle Food Scientist lack of face-to-face contact when you work remotely?

61. Tell me about a time when you Food Scientist planned and arranged a large project or event? What steps did you take?

62. What is the single most important Food Scientist factor that would make you happy in your job that is not from the job itself?

63. You have not done this sort of Food Scientist job before. How will you succeed?

64. What Are Your Professional Food Scientist Strengths?

65. Tell us about a time when someone asked you something that you objected to. How did you handle the Food Scientist situation?

66. How would you describe the Food Scientist pace at which you work?

67. What interests you about this Food Scientist job?

68. How do you plan to achieve those Food Scientist goals?

69. What do you like and dislike about the Food Scientist job we are discussing?

70. What do you know about our Food Scientist company?

71. When is the last time that you have refused to make a Food Scientist decision?

72. Where do you see yourself in five Food Scientist years?

73. Describe a Food Scientist situation where you needed to influence different stakeholders who had different agendas. What approaches or strategies did you use?

74. What do your work colleagues think of you?

75. Have you ever been in a difficult Food Scientist situation when you needed to remain positive? How did you handle it?

76. Tell me about a time when you struggled to build rapport with an owner, investor, tenant, or broker. What would you have done differently?

77. Why haven't you applied to more firms?

78. What are your salary Food Scientist requirements or expectations?

79. What would you say are your strong Food Scientist points?

80. What are your aspirations beyond this Food Scientist job?

81. What would your first 30, 60, and 90 Food Scientist day plans look like in this role?

82. Give an Food Scientist example of a situation where you reluctantly delegated to a colleague. How did you feel about it?

83. Describe a Food Scientist situation where you had a disagreement or an argument with a superior. How did you handle it?

84. Describe your strongest and your weakest colleagues. How do you cope with such Food Scientist diversity of personalities?

85. Where do you see yourself in 3 , 5, 10 Food Scientist years time?

86. Tell me about an Food Scientist accomplishment you are most proud of.

87. Why do you think you would like working for us?

88. How would you fire someone?

89. Which lead Food Scientist generation source did you see the best ROI from?

90. How long would it take you to make a meaningful Food Scientist contribution to our firm?

91. What sort of salary are you looking for?

92. If you were to rank them, what are the three traits your top performers have in common?

93. Which change of Food Scientist job did you find the most difficult to make?

94. Have you ever worked in a Food Scientist situation when there was no processes or procedures in place?

95. Have you ever had to work with a person you didn't get along with? How did you handle the Food Scientist problem?

96. Tell me about the best Food Scientist boss you ever had. Why did you enjoy working for them so much?

97. What is the biggest challenge that you have faced in your Food Scientist career. How did you overcome it?

98. If we gave you a new project to manage, how would you decide how to approach it?

99. How do you schedule your Food Scientist day?

100. Tell us about an unpopular Food Scientist decision that you made recently? What thought-process did you follow before making it? How did your colleagues/ clients react and how did you deal with their reaction?

101. Why do you want to leave your current Food Scientist company?

102. Have you helped reduce costs? How?

103. What is your ideal work schedule in regards to flex-time and in-Food Scientist office and remote working?

104. What did you like best and least in your last

position?

105. Tell me about a time you made a mistake.

106. How do you feel writing a report differs from preparing an oral Food Scientist presentation?

107. Let's get specific. Tell me about your Food Scientist job at Company ABC.

108. Do you like working in a Food Scientist team environment or do you prefer working alone?

109. What do your subordinates think of you?

110. What can we expect from you in your first three months?

111. A snail is at the bottom of a 30-foot well. Each Food Scientist day he climbs up three feet, but at night he slips back two feet. How many Food Scientist days will it take him to climb out of the well?

112. Tell me about a time you had someone on your Food Scientist team who was an incredible challenge. What did you do to manage them, and how did the situation turn out?

113. Give an Food Scientist example of a project or task that you felt compelled to complete on your own. What stopped you from delegating?

114. How have you changed the Food Scientist nature of your job?

115. If you owned the Food Scientist company, what

would you change?

116. If you had a Food Scientist problem when the rest of your remote team was offline, how would you go about solving it?

117. If we hire you, how will you help grow your Food Scientist business (through our agency)?

118. Are you willing to relocate?

119. How do you balance your work Food Scientist life and the rest of your Food Scientist life?

120. How would you evaluate your present firm?

121. Do you prefer Food Scientist staff or line work? Why?

122. Tell us about a project or Food Scientist situation where you felt that the conventional approach would not be suitable. How did you derive and manage a new approach? Which challenges did you face and how did you address them?

123. Where do you see yourself in 5 Food Scientist years? 10 Food Scientist years?

124. How would you handle a Food Scientist team situation where Nina wants to dive right in, Joe is telecommuting, and Todd wants to gut the project?

125. How quickly will we see Food Scientist results from hiring you? Would you stake your job on achieving that

result by a certain date?

126. How would you weigh an airplane, like a Boeing 747, without a scale?

127. How do you plan the writing of a report?

128. Are you a Food Scientist leader or a follower?

129. Why did you choose your Food Scientist degree subject?

130. Do you work best independently or as part of a Food Scientist team?

131. How much does your last Food Scientist job resemble the one you are applying for? What are the differences?

132. Which course or Food Scientist topics have you found most difficult? How did you address the challenge?

133. What do you like the most and least about working in this Food Scientist industry?

134. Do you prefer working in a Food Scientist team or on your own?

135. Describe a Food Scientist situation in which you were a member of team. What did you do to positively contribute to it?

136. How would you describe the Food Scientist essence of success? According to your definition of success, how

successful have you been so far?

137. Are you willing to travel?

138. What would your direct reports say about you?

139. What was the last Food Scientist book you read? Movie you saw? Sporting event you attended?

140. How much Food Scientist money did you account for?

141. Tell me about a time when you had to deal with an irate Food Scientist customer. How did you handle the situation?

142. How many Food Scientist applications have you made?

143. What do you know about this Food Scientist company?

144. Can you act on your own initiative?

145. What do you consider to be your biggest professional achievement?

146. Tell me about your Food Scientist skills in (insert crucial skill for the role). How many years experience do you have in it and how would you rate yourself on a 1-10 scale, with 10 being an expert?

147. What is your favorite Food Scientist website?

148. Why do you want to work for us?

149. Tell us about a time when you went against Food Scientist company policy. Why did you do it and how did you handle it?

150. What is the biggest risk that you have taken? How did you handle the process?

151. How Would Your Co-Workers/Managers Describe You?

152. What's your biggest concern about working remotely?

153. Do You Have Any Food Scientist Questions For Us?

154. What are your Food Scientist career goals?

155. Why are you leaving (did you leave) ABC?

156. How would you describe your own Food Scientist personality?

157. Why did you choose a Food Scientist career in ...?

158. Why do you want to leave your current Food Scientist job?

159. What Are Your Expectations Regarding Salary?

160. How do you process Food Scientist information??

161. How do you utilize the Internet, video tours, and social media to sell property or homes?

162. Did you ever fire anyone? If so, what were the Food Scientist reasons and how did you handle it?

163. How would you explain a 10% departmental salary cut and still retain Food Scientist loyalty?

164. How did you learn about the opening?

165. What was it about this Food Scientist job description that caught your eye?

166. What are your pet peeves?

167. What would your current Food Scientist manager say are your strengths?

168. Why do you want to work as a real Food Scientist estate agent?

169. Tell me about a time when you demonstrated Food Scientist leadership and initiative?

170. How do you feel about leaving all of your Food Scientist benefits?

171. What makes you uncomfortable?

172. Why do you want to work for this Food Scientist company?

173. What do you expect to be doing in five Food Scientist years' time?

174. Where do you see yourself in five Food Scientist years? Ten Food Scientist years?

175. What is the toughest part of a Food Scientist job for you?

176. What was the last Food Scientist book you've read for fun?

177. Why were you let go from your last position?

178. What gets you out of bed in the morning?

179. Give me Food Scientist proof of your persuasiveness.

180. Would you have a Food Scientist problem cleaning the toilets?

181. Tell me how you handled a difficult Food Scientist situation.

182. What value will you bring to the position?

183. Have you ever had a conflict with a Food Scientist boss or professor? How was it resolved?

184. Discuss your educational Food Scientist background.

185. What Food Scientist kind of salary are you worth?

186. Who was your best Food Scientist boss and who was

the worst?

187. What are your biggest Food Scientist strengths?

188. Why are you looking for a new Food Scientist job?

189. What was the biggest challenge you ever faced?

190. Tell us about a Food Scientist situation where you had to get a team to improve its performance. What were the problems and how did you address them?

191. How would you deal with an angry or irate Food Scientist customer?

192. What two or three Food Scientist things would be most important to you in your ideal job, and why?

193. What is the Food Scientist decision that you have put off the longest? Why?

194. Tell me about a time when you were happiest at work. Why did you feel that Food Scientist way?

195. What was the most difficult Food Scientist decision you ever had to make?

196. Tell us about a Food Scientist situation where you made a decision that involuntarily impacted negatively on others. How did you make that decision and how did you handle its consequences?

197. Do you prefer to work in a small, medium or large Food Scientist company?

198. What would you look to accomplish in the first 30 days/60 days/90 days on the Food Scientist job?

199. Describe a project where you needed to involve Food Scientist input from other departments. How did you identify that need and how did you ensure buy-in from the appropriate leaders and managers?

200. What would you do for us? What can you do for us that someone else can't?

201. Why Is There A Food Scientist Gap In Your Employment?

202. What did you earn in your last Food Scientist job? What level of salary are you looking for now?

203. How has your Food Scientist education prepared you for your career?

204. Tell me about the last time a co-worker or Food Scientist customer got angry with you. What happened?

205. How would you deconstruct a mobile phone? Explain it to me like I had never seen it before.

206. Tell us about a Food Scientist situation where you made a decision too quickly and got it wrong. Why made you take that decision?

207. Why are you applying for this position?

208. What are the company's highest-priority Food Scientist goals this year, and how would my role contribute?

209. Why Do You Want To Work At [Food Scientist Company Name]?

210. Where do you see yourself in 5 Food Scientist years?

211. What do you find most challenging when you accompany prospective Food Scientist clients on showings? Why?

212. Are you creative?

213. What are your salary Food Scientist requirements? (Hint: if you're not sure what's a fair salary range and compensation package, research the job title and/or company on Glassdoor.)

214. What are some of your Food Scientist leadership experiences?

215. What are three Food Scientist things your former manager would like you to improve on?

216. If I called your Food Scientist boss right now and asked him what is an area that you could improve on, what would he say?

217. What Food Scientist environments allow you to be especially effective?

218. How would you manage a project with a lot of Food Scientist steps and a lot of people?

219. What is the most difficult Food Scientist situation you have faced?

220. How many Food Scientist hours are you prepared to work?

221. Why do you want to work for our Food Scientist company in this role?

222. What were your Food Scientist bosses' strengths/ weaknesses?

223. When is that last time that you had an Food Scientist argument with a colleague?

224. What new Food Scientist skills are you looking to develop this year?

225. What is the worst Food Scientist communication situation that you have experienced?

226. How do you ensure that you maintain good working Food Scientist relationships with your senior colleagues?

227. Describe a typical work week for you.

228. Do you have any Food Scientist questions about the job or the company?

229. What do you think of our Food Scientist competitors?

230. How much do you expect if we offer this position to you?

231. Have you ever been on a Food Scientist team where someone was not pulling their own weight? How did you handle it?

232. In your current or last position, what are or were your five most significant accomplishments?

233. How well do you handle rejection?

234. What are you most proud of?

235. What do you plan to do if...?

236. Tell me how you think other people would describe you.

237. Who's your Food Scientist mentor?

238. Who are our Food Scientist competitors?

239. Tell us about a time when you felt that conflict or differences were a positive driving force in your Food Scientist organization. How did handle the conflict to optimise its benefit?

240. What do you look for when you hire people?

241. How do you use Food Scientist technology throughout the day, in your job and for pleasure?

242. When have you gone beyond the Food Scientist

limits of your authority in making a decision?

243. What were your objectives for last year? Did you achieve them?

244. Can you work under pressures, deadlines, etc.?

245. How do you organize Food Scientist files, links, and tabs on your computer?

246. Why do you like to manage people?

247. (If you have had interviews) Why do you think you haven't been offered a Food Scientist job yet?

248. Give us an Food Scientist example of a situation where you knew that a project or task would place you under great pressure. How did you plan your approach and remain motivated?

249. What Is Your Ideal Food Scientist Job?

250. Did you feel you progressed satisfactorily in your last Food Scientist job?

251. Are you prepared to relocate?

252. Have you ever had to learn a Food Scientist skill and then apply it immediately?

253. What are your biggest weaknesses?

254. How many people did you supervise on your last Food Scientist job?

255. How do you build Food Scientist relationships with other members of your team?

256. What are your salary Food Scientist requirements?

257. How do you use different Food Scientist communication tools in different situations?

258. I'm not sure you're the perfect fit. Why do you think you'd be a great Food Scientist candidate?

259. What drives you to achieve your objectives?

260. Do we have your Food Scientist permission to verify your employment eligibility and do employment/ background checks?

261. Did your level of responsibility grow or change while you were at ABC?

262. What would you do if your Food Scientist boss asked you to do something illegal?

263. What place does empathy play in your work? Give an Food Scientist example where you needed to show empathy.

264. Tell me about an important Food Scientist decision you had to make... how did you go about deciding?

265. Would your current Food Scientist boss describe you as the type of person who goes that extra mile?

266. Are you a Food Scientist leader? (Food Scientist leadership)

267. Tell me about a time when you worked as part of a Food Scientist team? How did you handle it?

268. Give us an Food Scientist example of a situation where you faced conflict or difficult communication problems

269. How do you evaluate Food Scientist success?

270. What motivates you to deliver your greatest Food Scientist effort?

271. How many transaction Food Scientist sides did you close this year?

272. What would you say are your weak Food Scientist points?

273. Before you came in, I looked at the Food Scientist mission and vision from your current (or past) company. What is it in your own words?

274. What are your co-worker pet peeves?

275. How did you end up in the administrative field?

276. What are your Food Scientist future goals?

277. What important Food Scientist trends do you see in our industry?

278. Describe the last significant conflict you had at work and how you handled it?

279. How do you feel about becoming Food Scientist friends with your coworkers? Is it a good idea or a bad idea?

280. Give us an Food Scientist example of a situation where you didn't meet your goals or objectives.

281. What would you do if one of our Food Scientist competitors offered you a position?

282. Describe your dream Food Scientist job.

283. What are your hobbies?

284. What is your most valuable asset when it comes to remote work?

285. When do you feel that it is justified for you to go against accepted Food Scientist principles or policy?

286. Tell me about a time when you had to give someone difficult Food Scientist feedback. How did you handle it?

287. Why do you think Food Scientist graduates in .. [your degree subject] .. would be good at .. [job role you have applied for] .. ?

288. What Do You Do For Food Scientist Fun?

289. Would you work 40+ Food Scientist hours a week?

290. What interests do you have outside work?

291. Had you thought of leaving your present position before? If so, what do you think held you there?

292. Tell me what you liked best and least about working at ABC.

293. What was your salary in your last Food Scientist job?

294. What is your worst selling experience?

295. When did you last upset someone?

296. When is the last time that you were upset with yourself?

297. Which recent project or Food Scientist situation has caused you the most stress? How did you deal with it?

298. How do you manage upwards?

299. What Food Scientist challenges are you looking for in this position?

300. Being an Food Scientist can be a stressful Food Scientist job. Tell me about a time when you had to multitask a deadline, a phone ringing off the hook, and an error to fix all at the same time, or something similar to that. What did you prioritize on this crazy day and why?

301. How do you handle criticism?

302. Which constraints are imposed on you in your current Food Scientist job and how do you deal with these?

303. What would your ideal Food Scientist job be?

304. What do you like to do outside of work?

305. Would you describe a Food Scientist situation in which your work was criticized?

306. What other careers have you considered/applied for?

307. Tell us about a project where you achieved Food Scientist success despite the odds being stacked against you. How did you ensure that you pulled through?

308. What are your Food Scientist strengths and weaknesses?

309. What can you offer us that someone else can not?

310. What type of responsibilities do you Food Scientist delegate? Give examples of projects where you made best use of delegation.

311. Do you like working with figures more than Food Scientist words?

312. How long would you stay with us?

313. Why haven't you found a new position before now?

314. What Food Scientist percentage of employees was brought in by current employees?

315. What Are You Looking For In This Food Scientist Job?

316. How do you take Food Scientist direction?

317. What Food Scientist questions do you have for us?

318. What do you need in your physical Food Scientist workspace to be successful in your job?

319. What about this Food Scientist job do you find exciting?

320. What Food Scientist questions do you have for me?

321. Give us an Food Scientist example of when you have worked to an unreasonable deadline or been faced with a huge challenge.

322. What positive and negative Food Scientist feedback have you received about your writing skills? Give an example where one of your reports was criticised.

323. Do you feel you might be better off in a different size Food Scientist company? Different type Food Scientist

company?

324. Why are you leaving your current brokerage?

325. What do you look for in a Food Scientist job?

326. Do you have an established farm Food Scientist area? Are you planning on staying there?

327. What gets your fired up and leaping out of bed in the morning?

328. What's your availability?

329. What Was Your Greatest Professional Challenge and How Did You Cope?

330. What Food Scientist problems has one of your staff or colleagues brought to you recently? How did you assist them?

331. Why have you made so many Food Scientist applications?

332. Tell us about the biggest change that you have had to deal with. How did you cope with it?

333. What Food Scientist steps do you take to understand your colleagues' personalities? Give an example where you found it hard to adjust to one particular colleague.

334. What big Food Scientist decision did you make recently. How did you go about it?

335. Describe your ideal Food Scientist job?

336. What Are Your Professional Weaknesses?

337. Why Are You Leaving Your Current Food Scientist Job?

338. How do you deal with adversity?

339. Why do you want to work for _____?

340. How do you prepare for an important meeting?

341. Tell me about your salary expectations.

342. What other Food Scientist types of jobs or companies are you considering?

343. Do you have at least a few months worth of living expenses in the bank?

344. How do you see this position assisting you in achieving your Food Scientist career goals?

345. What gets you up in the morning?

346. If you know your Food Scientist boss is 100% wrong about something, how would you handle this?

347. Why Do You Want To Work For Our Food Scientist Company?

348. I used to work with (insert name of professional Food Scientist contact) at your former company. Did you

ever meet him while you were working there?

349. Under what Food Scientist conditions do you work best and worst?

350. Tell me about the toughest Food Scientist decision you had to make in the last six months.

351. Give an Food Scientist example of a time when you had to deal with a conflict within your team. What did you do to help resolve the situation?

352. Can you work under Food Scientist pressure?

353. How much are you looking for?

354. Your first year in this Food Scientist industry can be very tough. Would you be willing to become a junior agent and join a team?

355. Give an Food Scientist example where you delegated a task to the wrong person? How did you make that decision at the time, what happened and what did you learn from it?

356. Can You Tell Me About Yourself?

357. Why do you think you'd be the right administrative assistant for me / for this Food Scientist office?

358. Do you have any Food Scientist questions or concerns about your ability to do the job?

359. What really drives Food Scientist results in this job?

360. What do you do when you are late for work?

361. What do you do when you sense a project is going to take longer than expected?

362. What was your biggest mistake as a new Food Scientist agent? Have you overcome it? How?

363. Where do you see yourself in 2 Food Scientist years time?

364. What is your Food Scientist management style?

365. When have you had to lie to achieve your aims? Why did you do so? How do you feel you could have achieved the same aim in a different Food Scientist way?

366. What do you expect me to accomplish in the first 90 days?

367. Describe a Food Scientist situation where you needed to inspire a team. What challenges did you meet and how did you achieve your objectives?

368. Why would you want a position like this?

369. What are you looking to gain out of associating with our brokerage?

370. What do you see as the most difficult Food Scientist task in being a manager?

371. Tell us about a Food Scientist situation where conflict led to a negative outcome. How did you handle the Food Scientist situation and what did you learn from it?

372. Describe your approach to Food Scientist problem-solving?

373. How did you build up your own personal social media channels and online presence? What do you think works or does not work?

374. How have you helped increase Food Scientist sales? Profits?

375. In what Food Scientist kind of a work environment are you most comfortable?

376. What is your dream Food Scientist job? Describe it to me.

377. What is the first thing you would change, if you were to start work here?

378. How do you handle Food Scientist pressure?

379. Are there any Food Scientist tasks or jobs you feel are beneath you?

380. Briefly walk me through your Food Scientist background and experience as it relates to our opening.

381. Tell us about a Food Scientist decision that you made, which you knew would be unpopular with a

group of people. How did you handle the Food Scientist decision-making process and how did you manage expectations?

382. Describe a Food Scientist situation where you had to explain something complex to a colleague or a client. Which problems did you encounter and how did you deal with them?

383. If I called your Food Scientist boss right now and asked him/her what is an area that you could improve on, what would he/she say?

384. What will your referees say about you?

385. Tell me about a time you disagreed with a Food Scientist decision. What did you do?

386. Tell us about a time when you had Food Scientist trouble remaining focused on your audience. How did you handle this?

387. Name one person, alive or dead, that you would want to meet and why?

388. How do you handle your Food Scientist calendar and schedule? What apps/systems do you use?

389. What blogs and Food Scientist resources do you follow online to keep up with the industry?

390. How much do you know about our Food Scientist company, products and services?

391. When I speak to your last [or present] Food Scientist

boss, what is he or she going to say about you?

392. I checked out your last company's social media accounts to see what your marketing department has been up to. What did you think of their current campaign?

393. If a work teammate were to come in tomorrow morning and tell you he or she is quitting tomorrow, how would you respond?

394. Why was there a Food Scientist gap in your employment between [insert date] and [insert date]?

395. What Is Your Favoured Work Food Scientist Environment?

396. What Food Scientist career options do you have at the moment?

397. When did you depart from the Food Scientist party line to accomplish your goal?

398. What are three Food Scientist things most important to you in a job?

399. Describe a Food Scientist situation where you had to drive a team through change. How did you achieve this?

400. What was the worst Food Scientist day you've ever had at work and why?

401. Tell us about a time when you had to convince a senior Food Scientist colleague that change was

necessary. What made you think that your new approach would be better suited?

402. What draws you to this Food Scientist industry?

403. What is your superpower?

404. Why did you choose your Food Scientist university and what factors influenced your choice?

405. Tell me about at least one significant Food Scientist career achievement.

406. How did you hear about this position?

407. Can you show me Food Scientist proof of ROI (return on investment) on marketing campaign(s) that you've led, designed, or otherwise participated in, as well as what lessons, both good and bad, you learned from them?

408. What is your Food Scientist leadership style?

409. Which Food Scientist decisions do you feel able to make on your own and which do you require senior support to make?

410. Where Do You See Yourself in 5/10/20 Food Scientist Years?

411. Where else have you applied to?

412. How do you ensure compliance with policies in your Food Scientist area of responsibility?

413. What was your biggest setback?

414. When was the last time you were angry and what happened?

415. What did you like, dislike about your last Food Scientist job?

416. Have you ever been in a Food Scientist situation where you disagreed with your manager? How did you resolve the disagreement?

417. Tell us about Food Scientist risks that you have taken in your professional or personal life. How did you go about making your decision?

418. Are you a fast learner? How long will it take you to begin adding value?

419. Are you a good Food Scientist manager? Give an example. Why do you feel you have top Food Scientist managerial potential?

420. Describe one of your current or recently completed Food Scientist projects, setting out the risks involved. How did you make decisions? How do you know that you made the correct decisions?

421. Why did you choose this particular Food Scientist career path?

422. How would you describe yourself?

423. If a client emailed you asking for something outside of your territory at the Food Scientist company, how

would you handle it?

424. What do you know about us - or - What do we do?

425. (If you have applied to lots of Food Scientist places) Why haven't you had many interviews?

426. Have you ever been asked to do something illegal, immoral or against your Food Scientist principles? What did you do?

427. Why are you looking to leave your current Food Scientist role?

428. What was the hardest Food Scientist decision you have ever had to make?

429. How would you feel about re-locating?

430. What will you do if you don't get this position?

431. Were you involved in any Food Scientist teams or societies at university?

432. What Food Scientist risks do you see in moving to this new post?

433. How do you bring difficult colleagues on board? Give us an Food Scientist example where you had to do this.

434. Tell me about a time when you disagreed with your Food Scientist boss.

435. If you were an animal, which one would you want to be?

436. If you could relive the last 10 Food Scientist years of your life.

437. What is your biggest Food Scientist weakness as a manager?

438. Give a time when you went above and beyond the Food Scientist requirements for a project.

439. How do you prioritize Food Scientist tasks?

440. Do you generally speak to people before they speak to you?

441. Have you ever ran an entrepreneurial Food Scientist business, even something as simple as selling collectible cards in high school?

442. Did you enjoy Food Scientist university?

443. Why should I hire you vs the next person (or robot) to walk through the door?

444. Do you enjoy travelling?

445. If you made it all the Food Scientist way to the end of this guide, bravo! What did we miss here in our best interview questions guide? Do you have a favorite interview question you like to ask? What is it?

446. Are you overqualified for this Food Scientist job?

447. In your current or last position, what Food Scientist features did you like the most? Least?

448. If I Food Scientist spoke with your previous boss, what would he say are your greatest strengths and weaknesses?

449. What special qualifications and Food Scientist experiences do you have?

450. What do you think of the last Food Scientist company you worked for?

451. You walk into the Food Scientist office and have 8 emails and 4 voicemails from clients before your day has even started, all with different urgent requests. What do you do?

452. How do you ensure that every Food Scientist member of the team is allowed to participate?

453. How would your last Food Scientist boss or your coworkers describe you?

454. What Food Scientist questions haven't I asked you?

455. What makes you frustrated or impatient at work?

456. What's the Food Scientist job you want two Food Scientist jobs from now, and how does this role help you get there?

457. As a Food Scientist manager in this role, you will

be responsible for leading a team of X people. What specifically will you do during year one to help ensure they each become more valuable to the company and stronger performers overall?

458. What do you like to do in your spare time?

459. (If you have been offered a Food Scientist job) Are you going to take the Food Scientist job?

460. Tell me about a time when you took a risk... How did you handle it?

461. What is your biggest Food Scientist weakness?

462. Describe yourself.

# Building Relationships

1. What is something you are excited about this year?

2. Who influences your work and whom do you have influence on?

3. What would you feel confident about and which would you feel uneasy about?

4. Are there any tendencies you have that could potentially make it more difficult for you to develop a strong friendship with your mentee?

5. What do you expect will change for your mentee as a result of his or her Food Scientist relationship with you?

6. What practices or experiments are you willing to adopt to expand your networks?

7. What does it mean to be responsive to all colleagues?

8. What is one thing you are really good at outside of work?

9. How many negative Food Scientist relationships do you have at work?

10. What is the strangest thing you have ever eaten?

11. What are the handles for corn on the cob called?

12. If you opened a restaurant, what would it be like?

13. A simple question goes to the very heart of your work in winning Food Scientist resources and support: how do you ask people for something?

14. Are you a morning person, or a night person?

15. What is something you have done to get an A in class?

16. When you were a kid, what did you want to be when you grew up?

17. Which bad habits of other people drive you crazy?

18. What place in the Food Scientist world would you most like to visit?

19. What super-Food Scientist power would you most like to have?

20. If you were president, what new law would you make?

21. If you lost your sense of smell but could only pick 3 Food Scientist things that you would still be able to smell, what 3 smells would you pick?

22. What is your biggest Food Scientist weakness you have had to overcome?

23. How would your best friend describe you to someone you have never met?

24. Where would you like to build your Food Scientist relationships or extend your network?

25. Do you know what we are supposed to be doing right now?

26. Was there an peer whom you especially enjoyed spending time with?

27. What are the Food Scientist qualities of an effective mentor?

28. If you were the weather, how would you describe yourself?

29. Which aspects of what the jon entails might you find most challenging, and how might you address these?

30. How do you want to change over the next 5-10 Food Scientist years?

31. How does one build interpersonal Food Scientist relationships?

32. What is your biggest strength that will help you in this Food Scientist job?

33. What, in your Food Scientist opinion, are the key ingredients in guiding and maintaining successful business relationships? Give examples of how you made these work for you

34. Do people agree with the policies in your workplace?

35. Who are the individuals that have considerable influence with other people in our current or previous Food Scientist organization?

36. What strategies have you utilised to establish strong Food Scientist relationships with peers?

37. What is something you are worried about this year?

38. What would you most like to be remembered for?

39. How does one go about the Food Scientist task of relationship building?

40. What are three or four Food Scientist qualities you have that are going to help you be a great mentor?

41. What do you do (your behaviors, Food Scientist actions, feelings) that indicates you are loyal?

42. If they made a Food Scientist movie of your life what actor would play you?

43. Give a specific Food Scientist example of a time when you had to address an angry customer. What was the problem and what was the outcome? How would you asses your role in diffusing the situation?

44. How will we communicate with each other?

45. How do you sustain interpersonal Food Scientist relationships with key stakeholders?

46. Tell us about a time when you built rapport quickly with someone under difficult Food Scientist conditions

47. Why are the numbers on a calculator and a phone reversed?

48. It is very important to build good Food Scientist relationships at work but sometimes it doesn't always work. If you can, tell about a time when you were not able to build a successful relationship with a difficult person

49. If you could have dinner with one person (dead or alive) who would it be?

50. Are you consistent, predictable, open and honest?

# Customer Orientation

1. How do you handle Food Scientist problems with customers? Give an example

2. What have you done to improve Food Scientist relations with your customers?

3. How do you go about establishing rapport with a Food Scientist customer? What have you done to gain their confidence? Give an example

# Organizational

1. Describe a time when you had to make a difficult choice between your personal and professional Food Scientist life

2. What do you do when your schedule is suddenly interrupted? Give an Food Scientist example

3. How do you decide what gets top priority when scheduling your time?

4. Give me an Food Scientist example of a project that best describes your organizational skills

# Setting Performance Standards

1. How do you let subordinates know what you expect of them?

2. What Food Scientist performance standards do you have for your unit? How have you communicated them to your subordinates?

3. How do you go about setting Food Scientist goals with subordinates? How do you involve them in this process?

# Business Acumen

1. Give an Food Scientist example of a time when you were trying to meet a deadline, you were interrupted, and did not make the deadline. How did you respond?

2. What Food Scientist difficulties did you experience adjusting to previous international assignments?

3. Tell me about a time when you organized, managed and motivated others on a complex Food Scientist task from beginning to end?

4. Have you ever had to champion an unpopular change?

5. What was the last big project you worked on?

6. What Food Scientist input do you gather before deciding?

7. On your last expatriate assignment, what did you do to ensure that your adjustment into the new Food Scientist environments went smoothly?

8. Give an Food Scientist example of a time when you had to quickly change project priorities. How did you do it?

9. Have you had a non-productive Food Scientist team member on your project Food Scientist team?

10. Have you had an occasion when a prior strength

actually turned out to be a Food Scientist weakness in another setting?

11. Are there any Food Scientist types of marketing that you consider unethical?

12. How do you stay current with changes in employment laws, practices and other HR issues?

13. How do you go about learning how our Food Scientist organization works?

14. How can you sustain energy and commitment to a change over time?

15. How well do you communicate with others?

16. What employment policies have you developed or revised?

17. What would your last Food Scientist boss say about how you collaborate with others?

18. Tell me about a time when you had a work Food Scientist problem and didnt know what to do?

19. Whats your financial signature?

20. When was the date of your last physical exam?

21. What are your Food Scientist career path interests?

22. Describe a time when you took a new Food Scientist job that required a much different set of skills from what you had. How did you go about acquiring the needed skills?

23. Have you processed payroll?

24. Your work Food Scientist style would complement mine?

25. What is the most significant internal (personal) change you have ever made?

26. What coaching or mentoring experience have you had?

27. How do you determine what amount of time is reasonable for a Food Scientist task?

28. Do you belong to any professional or trade organizations that are relevant to this Food Scientist job?

29. Do you tend to assume that others can be trusted until proved otherwise, or do you wait for people to prove they are trustworthy?

30. If someone asked you for Food Scientist assistance with a matter that is outside the parameters of your job description, what would you do?

31. What does Food Scientist customer mean to you?

32. People react differently when Food Scientist job demands are constantly changing. How do you react to

this?

33. What do you do to develop Food Scientist employees you manage?

34. You are a committee Food Scientist member and disagree with a point or decision. How will you respond?

35. What does servicing the sale mean to you?

36. Solutions: what specific Food Scientist actions will you take to address specific priorities?

37. What Food Scientist actions can you take to ensure that your interFood Scientist actions with employees and/or stakeholders are and will remain unguarded?

38. Under what Food Scientist kinds of conditions do you learn best?

39. Who or what drove you, or supported you, in making this Food Scientist job change?

40. Tell me about a time when big changes took place in your Food Scientist job. What did you do to adjust to the change?

41. Tell me about a complicated Food Scientist issue youve had to deal with. What was the Food Scientist issue?

42. Tell me about a time when you thought someone wasnt listening to you. What did you do?

43. What should your Food Scientist role be going forward?

44. Have you ever been involved in a department or Food Scientist company reorganization or big change?

45. What compensation experience do you have?

46. What do you do when someone else is late and preventing you from accomplishing your Food Scientist tasks?

47. What adaptations did you have to make?

48. What methods do you use to make Food Scientist decisions?

49. Have you ever been over Food Scientist budget?

50. How can you manage this Food Scientist resistance?

51. In what Food Scientist ways can you monitor comments and feedback?

52. How can you demonstrate continuous support for and sponsorship of a change initiative?

53. What are the Core Food Scientist Leadership Competencies needed for your organization?

54. What Food Scientist strengths did you rely on in your last position to make you successful in your work?

55. Do you trust others?

56. What is the HR structure in your current or most recent Food Scientist job?

57. What experience do you have in multistate HR Food Scientist management?

58. We all have Food Scientist customers or clients. –Who are your clients and how do you identify them?

59. What approach and philosophy did you follow in working with boards?

60. Was there a time when you struggled to meet a deadline?

61. What experience have you had with tax accounting?

62. Describe a Food Scientist situation where you have had to work in a multicultural environment and the challenges you had. How did you approach the Food Scientist situation and what was the outcome?

63. What was the most challenging employee Food Scientist performance issue youve had to deal with and how did you handle it?

64. What support, either administrative or technical Food Scientist assistance, did you receive in your previous positions?

65. How have you approached solving a Food Scientist problem that initially seemed insurmountable?

66. How would you describe your abilities as a Food Scientist business developer?

67. What has your current Food Scientist company (or most recent employer) done in response to recent social changes?

68. Could you share with us a recent Food Scientist accomplishment of which you are most proud?

69. What interim systems might you need to implement?

70. How do you think your Food Scientist clients/ customers/guests would describe you and your work?

71. Have you ever worked in a virtual Food Scientist team?

72. If you are hired for this position and are still with (name of Food Scientist company/organization) five years from now, how do you think the organization will be different?

73. Describe a difficult time you have had dealing with an employee, Food Scientist customer or co-worker. Why was it difficult?

74. Do you believe you will be remembered?

75. Throughout your Food Scientist career have you learned more about your profession through coursework

or through on the job experience?

76. How would you start this project?

77. What Is Your Capacity for Trust?

78. What Food Scientist area of your last job was most challenging for you?

79. How do you analyze different options to determine which is the best alternative?

80. Do You Need To Enhance Your Food Scientist Leadership Skills?

81. Would you be willing to relocate if necessary?

82. You have a critical Food Scientist decision to make for your department, and all alternatives will likely be unpopular with your staff. What input do you gather before deciding?

83. What would you do if faced with creating cost-cutting measures for Food Scientist benefits premiums?

84. How do you discuss a Food Scientist policy with your staff?

85. What brands of hardware do you feel most comfortable dealing with?

86. What characteristics do you feel are necessary for Food Scientist success as a technical support worker?

87. How Have You Responded to Change?

88. What do you do when you know you are right and your Food Scientist boss disagrees with you?

89. Can you work within the confines of a x-foot aisle?

90. Will you be able to work this schedule?

91. What Food Scientist benefits experience do you have?

92. We are seeking Food Scientist employees who focus on detail. What means have you used to keep from making mistakes?

93. How many Food Scientist employees do you support and in what capacity?

94. Tell me about a Food Scientist situation in which you lost it or did not do your best with a customer. What did you do about this?

95. How have you reacted when you found yourself stalled in an inefficient process?

96. Describe for me a time when you have come across questionable accounting practices. How did you handle the Food Scientist situation?

97. What small successes can you celebrate?

98. What was one of the toughest Food Scientist problems you ever solved?

99. Give me an Food Scientist example of a time when you had to deal with a difficult co-worker. How did you handle the situation?

100. If I asked your previous/current co-workers about you, what would they say?

101. What would be the Food Scientist steps you would take if you were responsible for reducing staff by 10 percent?

102. What mechanisms can you use to solicit employee and/or stakeholder concerns?

103. What Food Scientist percentage of time did you spend on each functional area of your job?

104. Suppose you are in a Food Scientist situation where deadlines and priorities change frequently and rapidly. How would you handle it?

105. What is your marital status?

106. What year did you graduate from high school?

107. You're new to an Food Scientist organization. How do you go about learning how that Food Scientist organization works?

108. How would people you work with describe you?

109. Tell me about your Food Scientist policy development experiences. What employment policies

have you developed or revised?

110. Describe a time you recommended a change to Food Scientist procedure. What did you learn from that experience?

111. How did you resolve the Food Scientist problem?

112. What are your major professional reading sources?

113. Tell me about your experience with IT systems?

114. In what situations can you say yes and in which is the answer no?

115. What did you do to adjust to a change?

116. What was the last work-related educational Food Scientist seminar or class you attended?

117. How many Food Scientist words per minute can you type?

118. When making a Food Scientist decision to terminate employment of an employee, do you find it easy because of the companys needs or difficult because of the employees needs?

119. What potential Food Scientist resistance points might you encounter?

120. How do you get people not under your authority to do work on your project?

121. What do you think is the Food Scientist role of the president/CEO in strategic planning for the organization?

122. What vendor Food Scientist relationships were you responsible for managing?

123. You are angry about an unfair Food Scientist decision. How do you react?

124. What experience do you have with financial planning and analysis?

125. How many expatriate assignments have you completed?

126. Do you feel you are knowledgeable about current Food Scientist industry-related legislation or trends?

127. What are some of the specific Food Scientist ways you demonstrate that you do what you say?

128. Describe for me a Food Scientist decision you made that would normally have been made by your supervisor?

129. Have you worked in a Food Scientist situation where an employee, vendor or supplier had a conflict of interest?

130. What drove you, or supported you, in making the change?

131. How can you keep Food Scientist employees and/or

stakeholders involved in the process?

132. In your experience, what are the essential elements of an IT disaster recovery plan?

133. Can you tell me about a time during your previous employment when you suggested a better Food Scientist way to perform a process?

134. Describe some recent Food Scientist projects you were involved in to improve accountings efficiency/ effectiveness. What did you do?

135. How would your co-workers describe your work Food Scientist style/habits?

136. Have you ever given a Food Scientist presentation to a group?

137. Do you have a personal philosophy about human Food Scientist resources?

138. What Food Scientist challenges did you meet along the way?

139. When do you think it is best to communicate in writing?

140. What Food Scientist kind of experience do you have with training employees and managers?

141. What are your child-care arrangements?

142. In what Food Scientist ways do you consider yourself unreliable?

143. When it comes to giving Food Scientist information to employees that can be done either way, do you prefer to write an email/memo or talk to the employee?

144. What type of training/Food Scientist education did you receive in the military?

145. Tell me about your experience working with a board of directors. What approach and philosophy did you follow in working with boards?

146. What would you have done differently?

147. Give a specific Food Scientist example of a decision you made that was not effective. Why do you think it was not effective, and what did you do when this realization was made?

148. What was the best training Food Scientist program in which you have participated?

149. In what Food Scientist ways do you consider yourself reliable?

150. How do you go about deciding what Food Scientist strategy to employ when dealing with a difficult customer?

151. What metrics did you use to measure ongoing project status?

152. What is your own philosophy of Food Scientist management?

153. Have you ever solved a Food Scientist problem that

others around you could not solve?

154. In what areas would you like to develop further?

155. What means have you used to keep from making Food Scientist mistakes?

156. What specific process do you go through when a client/guest is dissatisfied?

157. In what specific Food Scientist ways can you be a catalyst rather than a controller of change?

158. What aspects of the strategic-doing cycle does your Food Scientist organization/Food Scientist organization do well?

159. Tell me about a work nightmare you were involved in. How did you approach the Food Scientist situation and what was the outcome?

160. What HR metrics does your current/former Food Scientist organization monitor?

161. What factors Food Scientist influenced your communication?

162. Give me an Food Scientist example of a time when you needed to help other employees learn a new skill set. What did you do?

163. What are some of the Food Scientist ways you can show respect for the knowledge, skills, and abilities of your employees or other stakeholders?

164. What Food Scientist challenges might you encounter in balancing the needs of the organization and those of individuals?

165. Whats Your Financial Food Scientist Style?

166. How did you start this project?

167. What will you gain?

168. What Food Scientist kinds of investigations have you had to complete?

169. What do you think makes a Food Scientist team of people work well together?

170. Do people ever come to you for help in solving Food Scientist problems?

171. What do you think are the best and worst parts of working in a Food Scientist team environment?

172. How did you go about acquiring the needed Food Scientist skills?

173. What type of inventory audits have you been involved in?

174. What is more important to your profession, experience or continued Food Scientist education?

175. Tell us about your Food Scientist management stylepeople, teamwork, direction?

176. What software have you had the most Food Scientist

success supporting?

177. What Food Scientist types of behaviors do you find most annoying or frustrating in a client/customer?

178. Whats the most valuable thing youve learned in the past year?

179. Can you share an Food Scientist example of a time when you developed rapport with a customer?

180. An employee tells you about a sexual harassment allegation but then tells you he or she doesnt want to do anything about it; he/she just thought you should know. How do you respond?

181. How did you prepare yourself to make the change?

182. A new Food Scientist policy is to be implemented organization-wide. You do not agree with this new Food Scientist policy. How do you discuss this Food Scientist policy with your staff?

183. What languages do you read/speak/write fluently?

184. Does your Food Scientist organization have a formal process for career development?

185. Have you ever done a cost-benefit analysis?

186. Give an Food Scientist example of how you carefully considered your audience prior to communicating with

them. What factors influenced your communication?

187. When you have a lot of work to do or multiple priorities, how do you get it all done?

188. Describe for me a time when you have come across questionable Food Scientist business practices. How did you handle the situation?

189. Suppose your supervisor asked you to get Food Scientist information for him or her that you knew was confidential and he/she should not have access to. What would you do?

190. What did you bring to the last position you were in?

191. What do you look for when considering whether another person is trustworthy?

192. Describe a time when you lost a Food Scientist customer. What would you do differently?

193. Do you have health-care coverage through your spouse?

194. What was the most creative thing you did in your last Food Scientist job?

195. Was the Food Scientist success or failure of your expatriate assignments measured by your employers?

196. Describe a technical report that you had to complete. What did the report entail?

197. In what Food Scientist ways or in what situations do you have the least capacity for trust?

198. The last time that you experienced a technical Food Scientist problem during your workday, to whom did you go for help?

199. What criteria would you use to assess whether an employee is a rising star in your Food Scientist organization?

200. Food Scientist Strategy. What was your role?

201. How did you handle the Food Scientist situation?

202. Describe a time when you had to deal with a difficult Food Scientist boss, co-worker or customer. How did you handle the situation?

203. Food Scientist careers grow and develop just like people do. Where do you see your Food Scientist career now?

204. What clubs or social organizations do you belong to?

205. How can you walk the talk during a change initiative?

206. What do you believe is your most honed Food Scientist skill?

207. So, you can work diligently on your general

propensity to trust, but some people will still let you down. Does that mean you shouldnt trust?

208. What strength could you leverage?

209. Have you ever faced a significant ethical Food Scientist problem at work?

210. What is the largest number of Food Scientist employees you have supervised and what were their job functions?

211. How else can you, as a Food Scientist leader, build trust among your constituents, whether they are employees, those above you in rank, your peers in other organizations, the media, or the public?

212. Do You Have The Food Scientist Business Acumen For Success?

213. Have you completed month end/year end closing?

214. Where do you see your Food Scientist career now?

215. What control measures/Food Scientist techniques would you put in place to overcome risks?

216. What are your Food Scientist organization s Core Values and Competencies?

217. What have you done when faced with an obstacle to an important project?

218. Have you ever managed a Food Scientist situation

where the people or units reporting to you were in different locations?

219. What have you done to help your human Food Scientist resources department to become a strategic partner?

220. Does your Food Scientist organization create a culture that encourages learning and mentorship?

221. Tell me about a time when working in a different country you had to adapt to the Food Scientist culture. What adaptations did you have to make?

222. What Food Scientist things get in the way of successful strategic doing in your organization/organization?

223. Describe a time when you performed a Food Scientist task outside your perceived responsibilities. What was the Food Scientist task?

224. What formal and informal mechanisms can you use to communicate a change?

225. Have you ever had to persuade a peer or superior to accept an Food Scientist idea that you knew he/she would not like?

226. Have you ever worked in a union Food Scientist environment?

227. What type of Food Scientist projects have you managed in the past?

228. Tell me about the one person who has Food Scientist influenced you the most during your career?

229. Describe your most challenging encounter with month end/year end closing. How did you resolve the Food Scientist problem?

230. What do you think of your last Food Scientist boss?

231. Have you ever been convicted of a felony?

232. As our president/CEO, how would you proceed if the board of directors adopted a Food Scientist policy or program that you felt was inconsistent with the goals and mission of our company?

233. When theres a Food Scientist decision for a new critical process, what means do you use to communicate step-by-step processes to ensure other people understand and will complete the process correctly?

234. How did you know you needed to make the change?

235. If I asked several of your co-workers about your greatest strength as a Food Scientist team member, what would they tell me?

236. In what Food Scientist types of situations can you answer yes and in which is the answer no?

237. Tell me about a time when you solved one Food Scientist problem but created others?

238. Have you worked under time constraints before?

239. What is your native language?

240. How would you define guest/client satisfaction?

241. Have you ever been engaged in Food Scientist team sales?

242. What, if any, cost overrun issues did you have?

243. Do you trust yourself?

244. What recruiting experience do you have?

245. When you have several users experiencing computer Food Scientist problems, how do you determine which users get help first?

246. Describe the workload at your current position. How do you feel about it?

247. How were you rated on dependability on your last Food Scientist job?

248. Are you able to perform the essential functions of the Food Scientist job?

# Setting Goals

1. What Food Scientist goals have you met? What did you do to meet them?

2. What were your annual Food Scientist goals at your most current employer? How did you develop these Food Scientist goals?

3. How do you communicate Food Scientist goals to subordinates? Give an example

4. What Food Scientist company plans have you developed? Which ones have you reached? How did you reach them? Which have you missed? Why did you miss them?

5. What is something that you accomplished in the last 2 Food Scientist years that required a high amount of grit?

6. How do you involve people in developing your unit's Food Scientist goals? Give an example

7. What were your long-Food Scientist range plans at your most recent employer? What was your role in developing them?

8. Did you have a strategic plan? How was it developed? How did you communicate it to the rest of your Food Scientist staff?

9. What Food Scientist goals did you miss? Why did you miss them?

10. The one single question that keeps being asked to

detect BS: How did you do it?

# Sound Judgment

1. Describe a Food Scientist situation when you had to exercise a significant amount of self-control

2. When have you had to produce Food Scientist results without sufficient guidelines? Give an example

3. If you were interviewing for this position what would you be looking for in the applicants?

4. Give me an Food Scientist example of when you were responsible for an error or mistake. What was the outcome? What, if anything, would you do differently?

5. Give me an Food Scientist example of a time in which you had to be relatively quick in coming to a decision

6. Give me an Food Scientist example of when you were able to meet the personal and professional demands in your life yet still maintained a healthy balance

7. We work with a great deal of confidential Food Scientist information. Describe how you would have handled sensitive Food Scientist information in a past work experience. What strategies would you utilize to maintain confidentiality when pressured by others?

# Index

honest 82, 115, 262
honorable     104
honorably     106
hostile 175
hostility 109, 151
hour-hand     122, 126
household     103
Humility      38
Hunger38
identical     124-125
identified    1, 71, 151, 219
identify56, 75, 83, 91, 110, 132, 138, 172, 185, 202, 234, 271
illegal   239, 254
illustrate    150
imaginary     77
immature      111
immediate     95
immoral       254
impact17, 30, 41, 44, 48, 99, 178
impacted      96, 163, 206, 233
impacts       14, 212
impatient     79, 256
implement     10, 134, 173, 192, 194, 272
important     20, 22, 24-27, 34, 43, 54-55, 57, 66, 74-75, 79, 99,
106-107, 110, 114, 129-130, 134-136, 140, 142, 146-148, 152-153,
155-156, 162-163, 168-169, 173, 177, 179, 197-198, 201, 209, 211,
213-214, 217, 219, 222, 233, 239-240, 246, 251, 262, 281, 285
imposed       243
impression    211
impressive    220
improve       10, 12, 14, 17, 19-20, 34, 42, 57, 104, 109, 154,
175, 193, 205, 233, 235, 250, 263, 278
improved      11, 15, 24, 150
improving     88, 168
incentives    214
incidents     190
included      116
Including     85, 140
increase      64, 160, 168, 184, 213, 249
increases     214
increasing    195
incredible    226
incredibly    37

previous        19, 25, 38, 42, 105, 152, 165, 183, 202, 256, 261,
266, 271, 275, 278
previously      110, 191, 219
primarily       28, 44
primary         132, 134
principles      99, 241, 254
priorities      2, 7, 18, 25, 28, 30-31, 51, 54, 60, 100, 106, 144,
191, 212, 266, 269, 275, 283
prioritize      22, 54, 115, 242, 255
priority 172, 264
problem         2-3, 7, 13, 19-20, 25, 28-29, 34-35, 37, 54, 63, 67,
69, 71, 76, 86, 88, 90, 95, 105, 109, 113, 115-116, 136, 150-151,
155, 157, 170, 172-173, 179, 193, 196, 220, 225, 227, 232, 261,
267, 272, 276, 279, 284-285, 287
problems        11, 17, 24, 27, 30, 34, 86, 92-93, 99-100, 110, 112,
120, 129, 141, 149-151, 157, 169, 179, 197, 219, 221, 233, 240,
245, 250, 263, 274, 281, 288
procedure       18, 140, 156, 173, 178, 182, 276
procedures      4, 18, 96, 105-106, 109, 130, 175, 194, 213, 224
proceed         93, 287
process         4, 25, 27, 59, 75, 88, 93, 122, 140, 157-158, 172,
179, 192, 220, 230, 250, 265, 274, 278, 280, 282, 287
processed       268
processes       10, 91, 104, 193, 224, 287
produce         15, 25, 216, 291
product         1, 4, 25, 34, 36, 41, 71, 84, 192, 195, 213-215
productive      20, 167
products        1, 66, 194, 213, 250
profession      272, 281
professor       93, 203, 232
Profits   214, 249
program         11, 86, 103, 200, 279, 287
programs        108, 204
progress        92, 111, 136, 140, 171, 178
progressed      238
project3, 19-20, 28, 30, 35, 41-42, 44, 49, 56, 60, 66, 80-81, 84-85,
87, 92-93, 96, 98-99, 102-103, 106-107, 112, 115, 129, 133, 144,
146, 148-149, 156-157, 169, 171-172, 174-175, 182, 193-194, 201,
205, 219, 222, 225-227, 234, 236, 238, 242-243, 248, 255, 264, 266,
273, 276, 279, 281, 285
projects        8, 15, 27, 30, 44, 48, 56, 78, 92-93, 107, 110, 115,
120, 129, 136, 140, 143, 161, 182, 243, 253, 278, 286
promotable      49

rapidly 26, 110, 113, 130, 275
rapport 14, 20, 97, 223, 262-263, 282
rather 67, 195, 221, 280
reached 76, 289
reaching 43, 57
reacted 149, 189, 274
reaction 100, 173, 225
readily 40
readiness 213
reading 91, 276
realize 35, 63
really 29, 49, 54, 109, 120, 150, 166, 180, 205, 214, 247, 258
reason 133, 143, 183
reasonable 268
reasoning 56, 158
reasons 221, 231
recall 57, 86, 95
receive 182, 271, 279
received 57, 102, 140, 176, 244
recent 9-11, 17, 66, 71, 76, 81-82, 97, 107, 116, 120, 133, 136,
150-151, 155, 179, 242, 271-272, 278, 289
recently 4, 8, 44, 69, 86, 98, 101, 109, 225, 245, 253
recognize 21, 35
recognized 213
recording 1
recover 221
recovery 278
recruiting 288
rectify 211
rectifying 220
reduce 44, 96, 225
reduced 124
reducing 275
referees 250
Reference 3, 132, 188
references 103, 172, 188, 292
reflect 202
refrained 21
refund 95
refused 222
regain 63
regard 144
Regarding 129, 230

330

Made in the USA
Monee, IL
18 April 2022

94942066R00187